Book One
of the

Paid in Full

Financial Series

Radical Trust
In God
For Finances

Roger Sapp

Order this book and the companion volumes from:

ISBN: 0-9702341-3-9

All Nations Publications
P.O. Box 92847
Southlake, Texas 76092
United States of America
1-817-514-0653

Beyond a Shadow of a Doubt, Doubts that block healing.
Performing Miracles and Healing, Christ-like ministry.
The Last Apostles on Earth, Modern apostolic ministry.
Apostolic Fathers & Spiritual Bastards, A heresy reviewed.
Pandora's Pulpit, Women's ministries & apostolic government.

Booklets:
Honoring the Truth-teller, Loyalty & truthfulness balanced.
Beware of Spiritual Wolves, Wolf-packs & false ministers.
The Subtle Spirit of Antichrist, Winds & trends in the last days.
Genetics, Homosexuals and the Bible, Bible teaching & trends.
Receive the Holy Spirit's Power, Baptism in the Holy Spirit.
Make No Covenant, Christian covenant-making reviewed.

Printed in the United States by Morris Publishing
3212 East Highway 30 • Kearney, NE 68847
1-800-650-7888

Paid in Full

Book One
Radical Trust in God for Finances

Introduction

This is the first of a series of books on the subject of Christ-centered New Testament finances. Originally, I thought that I might write a single comprehensive book on this subject. However, as my preparations to write continued and the writing began, I realized that there was much more to this subject in the New Testament than I had originally anticipated. Indeed, there may be more verses in the New Testament devoted to the subject of money than any other single subject. Prayerfully, I decided that several smaller books would be easier for readers to digest the great volume of instruction concerning money in the New Testament.

The failure to proclaim all Christ's words on money is the primary reason that most people in the Church experience very little in the way of the supernatural in their finances. Even those churches that have been criticized for prosperity teaching and for having an emphasis on money seem to neglect a great deal of what the New Testament reveals on the matter of money.

This book begins with foundational matters and then focuses upon the most neglected truths in the teaching of Jesus Christ concerning finances. My study of finances was often prompted by usual experiences of obeying the Holy Spirit that resulted in great financial blessing. In other words, I believe that the Holy Spirit led me to these truths by experience.

These neglected New Testament truths on finances are what this series of books seeks to present. Each book will build upon the previous book. Therefore, I ask the reader to be patient as I try to present this large volume of scriptural material in a wise way. No single book will answer all the questions someone might have but will be part of a whole. The other books will cover these major subjects and other related subjects that are not listed here:

Christ's miracles of supply, financial support of the Twelve apostles and today's minister, support for the poor, Paul's instruction to Timothy on money, Paul's attitude towards financial support, the Great Collection for the Jewish poor believers in Paul's day, betraying the cause of Christ for money, governmental taxation, comparison of the Old Covenant financial system with the New Covenant financial system, an explanation of the three Christian views on tithing and a very detailed look at the pros and cons of tithing.

I believe that if we fully understand the financial teaching of Jesus Christ, His Twelve apostles and later apostles such as Paul and James, the Lord's brother, then we will be able to please the Lord in this very important area and see His blessing. To the end of pleasing the Lord, I humbly submit this first book for your study.

For the Bridegroom and His preparing Bride,

Roger Sapp

~1~

Foundations for Biblical Finances

The foundations of biblical finances are tied very closely to a particular truth. Those who do not understand this truth very well often neglect this matter in public teaching. They may use the words that the Bible uses in financial matters but the truth behind these words is misunderstood, underestimated and often unapplied in their own lives. The neglecting of this truth is often the reason why many attempting to follow Christ in the arena of finances see little evidence that He is pleased. They see little evidence of a supernatural touch on their finances in an ongoing way. *What is this particular truth that is neglected and missing?* By telling the reader in a direct way, we quickly invite the reader to turn off their attention because they may think that they already understand this underestimated truth. However, it is clear that the many maturing believers do not understand this truth and are not living in it at all. Therefore, this text will first outline what this truth means before identifying the concept to avoid this problem. Then we will discuss aspects of this foundational truth in the following outline in various portions of this book. Here is an outline of this foundational concept of biblical finances.

- God owns all things. This includes the physical universe and all spiritual beings good and bad. God's ownership includes planet Earth, all living things, the people, their ideas, their gifts and capacities and all the world's wealth, hidden and revealed.
- We actually own nothing. The righteous angels, the devil, all fallen angels and demons also own nothing.
- The idea of human ownership is a powerful deception. Actually, all we really have is temporary possession and control of the things that God owns.
- God requires us to be responsible and account for how we handle His property that He places in our control.
- We owe nothing to God but thanks because Christ has paid for our indebtedness at Calvary.
- Failure to understand the above concepts and to consistently apply them produces inadequate resources.
- The world's system of finance is built on the human responses that a lack of adequate resources creates; chiefly fear in the form of anxiety and greed.
- God's financial system is higher than the world's financial system. It is built on hidden abundance. Most of God's resources are hidden in Christ but available to all who wish to walk as Christ's servants in finances.
- Entering into God's system of finances requires faith in Christ and releases abundant resources and the inner quality of peace.
- Giving all resources away on command of Christ reveals a true application of spiritual financial understanding. Failure to pass this test is why many do

4

not experience the supernatural in finances. This is a key concept that is neglected in most teaching on finances. Absence of this concept produces financial teaching that appears shallow, greedy and selfish.

- God entrusts His things and His wealth to Christ's special tested servants who are genuinely and acutely aware that they own nothing. They are properly called *stewards*.

- A faithful and tested *steward* will see ongoing supernatural increase and unusual supernatural intervention by Christ in his or her finances.

- The lifestyle that lives by the truth that God owns all things and human beings own nothing is then called *stewardship*.

Perhaps you can see why we didn't use the word *stewardship* in the beginning of this chapter. The word has often been misunderstood and therefore misused and has come to mean something much less than its biblical meaning. The word *stewardship* has been used often only in reference to financial support of local churches and ministries, but it has a much greater and important meaning.

The Meaning of Stewardship
The word *steward* or forms of this word are used frequently in the New Testament. The Greek word translated *steward* is *oikonomos* which is a composite word coming from *oikos* meaning *house* and *nemo* meaning *arrange*. The literal meaning of the word is *the one who arranges the house*. The word in the First Century denoted a manager of a household or estate. These managers or

5

stewards were slaves or freemen but were never owners of the property that they managed. Christ in the Gospels and Paul and Peter in their letters in the New Testament use the words *steward* and *stewardship* metaphorically to describe the believer's relationship to various things.[1]

Christ and the Stewardship Parables

Several of Christ's parables are about stewards. In each case the owner or master represents God or Christ and the steward, a servant or slave, represents each believer. There are some today who would react to this truth of servanthood or stewardship on the basis of sonship. They might reason that we are sons and daughters of God and not His servants. This is partly true and partly false. Our sonship does not negate the fact that we are still called as servants, as bond-slaves, of Christ. We must hold these truths in balance. We are the children of God and the servants of Christ, our Savior and our Lord. Despite the fact that we have the same Father, Christ is still King of Kings and Lord of Lords. We are properly the servants, the stewards, of our gracious elder brother, Jesus Christ. While this relationship may take a different form in the age to come, presently it is true. Therefore, Christ teaches us from the Gospels about what He expects of His stewards. For instance, Luke records Christ in this way:

> *Now He was also saying to the disciples, "There was a certain rich man who had a **steward**, and this **steward** was reported to him as squandering his possessions. Luke 16:1*

---

[1] The Expanded Vine's Expository Dictionary of New Testament Words, pg. 1087 *Steward, Stewardship*

The basic concept of stewardship is revealed here. The rich man representing God is the owner. The steward, representing a Christian, has control over the owner's possessions and in this case is squandering them. Christ calls this steward an *unrighteous steward* later in this passage. *Why?* The steward was supposed to be taking good care of the owner's property and was not. We will return to this passage later in this book for an examination of the financial teaching of Christ in this passage. For now, we will be content with revealing the concept of stewardship. In another place, Christ uses the concept of a steward to represent the Christian in this manner:

> *And the Lord said, "Who then is the faithful and sensible **steward**, whom his master will put in charge of his servants, to give them their rations at the proper time? Blessed is that **slave** whom his master finds so doing when he comes. Truly I say to you, that he will put him in charge of all his possessions. "*
> *Luke 12:42-43*

The context of Christ's statement is in a passage where Christ is teaching on His second coming. He reveals several important truths in these verses about stewards. Here they are:

- There is an implicit expectation in these verses that all believers would understand that they are stewards.
- A good steward is expected to be faithful and sensible.
- The Master (Christ) puts a steward in charge of His people and His resources.

7

- Those resources are to be used to care for Christ's other servants.
- A steward is a servant. Likewise, all slaves or servants should be good stewards. The two concepts of service and stewardship are intertwined and are frequently found together in the New Testament.
- The steward is expected to continue to serve faithfully until his Master returns.
- On returning, the Master will promote a faithful steward with more resources and people to care for.

You should be able to see how important and neglected the concept of stewardship is. It is the missing foundation under much of the teaching on finances that is heard in the Church today. Its absence is why some teaching on finances doesn't ring true and sounds shallow and greedy. We will return to this statement of Christ later in this book since it is in a context that explains what will happen with a steward who is not faithful. The statement also follows a passage where Christ is doing some direct financial teaching. For now we will be content in revealing the basic truth of stewardship.

The Apostle Paul and Stewardship
The apostle Paul wrote much in regard to stewardship. He clearly saw it in a larger context than just finances but certainly included finances. For instance, Paul's advice to Titus about appointing overseers includes the concept of stewardship. Paul wrote:

> For the **overseer** must be above reproach as God's **steward**, not self-willed, not quick-tempered, not

addicted to wine, not pugnacious, not fond of sordid gain, Titus 1:7

Paul is revealing here is that an overseer or elder in the Church must see the individual believers and the resources of the Church that he cares for as a stewardship from Christ. He cannot somehow think or act as if he somehow he owns the people and the financial resources that God places in His hands. Paul's rejection criteria for overseers are mainly poor character qualities that would disqualify them from taking good care of people. Being self-willed, quick-tempered, alcoholic, and pugnacious[2] are negative character qualities that would prevent a man from properly taking care of people. He would harm them rather than help them. Paul also tells Titus to reject a man for leadership if he is too fond of money and doesn't care much about how he obtains the money. This poor character quality would preclude a man from taking good care of the financial resources of a fellowship of believers. He might even abuse the people of faith to obtain money and fail in proper stewardship of both and bring reproach to the Gospel.

The apostle Paul often used the concept of stewardship to describe his service to Christ. Here the twin concepts of servant and steward are revealed together by Paul:

*Let a man regard us in this manner, as **servants** of Christ, and **stewards** of the mysteries of God. In this case, moreover, it is required of **stewards** that one be found trustworthy. 1 Corinthians 4:1-2*

---

[2] Pugnacious means argumentative, quick to enter a conflict.

It is clear that Paul understood that as a servant of Christ he had been given a stewardship. In this case, Paul tells us *the mysteries of God* were given to him as a stewardship. This was something that he did not own but he was a manager over. He was required by God to care properly for these *mysteries* by being *trustworthy*. Paul mentioned this stewardship several other times. For instance, he writes a few chapters later in the same book:

> *For if I preach the gospel, I have nothing to boast of, for I am under compulsion; for woe is me if I do not preach the gospel. For if I do this voluntarily, I have a reward; but if against my will, I have a **stewardship** entrusted to me. What then is my reward? That, when I preach the gospel, I may offer the gospel without charge, so as not to make full use of my right in the gospel. 1 Corinthians 9:16-18*

Here Paul tells us that the stewardship entrusted to him is preaching the gospel. He reveals several truths about stewards in these verses. First of all, stewards who *voluntarily* serve the Master are rewarded by Him and have resources to use for their personal support. Stewards who do not serve voluntarily are still required to serve and to be accountable to the master but have no reward of personal resources. They remain servants and slaves to the master no matter what their attitude and still must account to the Master. Paul was able to preach the gospel freely without recompense because he was a good steward being rewarded by God with resources coming from other means than preaching the gospel.[3] Paul also revealed his stewardship in Ephesians, Chapter 3. There he writes:

> *For this reason I, Paul, the prisoner of Christ Jesus for the sake of you Gentiles--if indeed you have heard of the **stewardship** of God's grace which was given to me for you... Ephesians 3:1*

Paul calls his stewardship here a *stewardship of God's grace*. He also reveals that the stewardship is *for you*. In other words, he must use this stewardship to help people in the household of faith. In Colossians, Paul reveals a similar truth. He writes:

> *Of this church I was made a minister according to the **stewardship** from God bestowed on me for your benefit, that I might fully carry out the preaching of the word of God... Colossians 1:25*

Paul's stewardship was bestowed from God for their benefit. In the earlier passages, Paul told us of a stewardship of God's mystery, of preaching the Gospel, of grace and now, the preaching of the Word of God. Of course, these are the same stewardship described by Paul in various ways. In other words, Paul's ministry to others, his service, was a stewardship to God. He did not own it. It remained God's property and he must account to God for how he served others as a steward.

---

[3] Paul also asserts that support from the Gospel was his right as other ministers. However, he was "boasting" that he didn't have to resort to this right.

The Apostle Peter and Stewardship
The apostle Peter tells us that we are stewards in the same manner as Paul. He writes:

As each one has received a special gift, employ it in serving one another, as good stewards of the manifold grace of God. 1 Peter 4:10

Here Peter tells us that each of us has a gift to serve each other. The gifts are not ours; they have been *received*. They belong to God because they come through a stewardship of the grace of God. We are expected by God to use that which we have been given faithfully and sensibly to serve Christ as we serve others.

Conclusion
We need to see this truth in all its facets. Everything that we have been given belongs to God. We have a stewardship of people given to us. Our husband or wife and our young children are given to us as stewardship from God for a season. We are to use the other resources that God has given to us to care for them. Our brothers and sisters in Christ are a stewardship. All our financial resources and physical property are a stewardship from God. All our gifts, ministries and vocations, spiritual and natural, are stewardships from God. He expects us to be faithful and sensible in our care of all these things and return them faithfully to Him when the time arrives. This time of accountability will quickly come, either at Christ's return or our own deaths. Therefore, we have no time to waste in learning about what the Master wishes in stewardship. Therefore, in the next chapter, we will begin

12

to review the wonderful teachings of the Lord Jesus Christ on stewardship and finances. Since the Church has neglected to teach much of this, there will surely be a few surprises to most readers.

~2~

Sell All, Give All, Leave All

The weakest area of understanding about biblical finances in the North American Church is the actual lifestyle of New Testament stewardship. Because few are living this lifestyle, there are few that can teach it to others. In turn, this means that the wisdom of this lifestyle is practically unknown throughout the North American Church. This causes this message to sound strange and radical when someone teaches it. However, the Holy Spirit strongly witnesses to the truth within the hearts of the children of God when they hear Christ's words presented in a faithful way.

Christ's Radical Message on Finances

Indeed Christ's message on finances is strange and radical to the world's way of thinking. However, embracing the message creates great blessing. The Lord Jesus taught us about the radical nature of stewardship in two short parables. Matthew records Christ saying:

*The kingdom of heaven is like a treasure hidden in the field, which a man found and hid; and from joy over it he goes and **sells all** that he has, and buys that field. Again, the kingdom of heaven is like a merchant seeking fine pearls, and upon finding one pearl of great value, he went and **sold all** that he had and bought it. Matthew 15:44-46*

Both of these parables describe the rule of God coming to a believer. That believer discovers something wonderful and of great value and *sells all* that he owns to obtain it. The treasure to be obtained is Christ Himself. Those who discover the truth of stewardship also must *sell all* that they own to obtain the treasure of Christ. In their hearts, they must *sell all* that which cannot produce life to obtain the One who is life. Emotionally, they must release resources that cannot produce security to obtain the One who is security. They must release that which doesn't really belong to them at all and enter into deeper relationship with Christ who is their life. This is a call to radical trust in what Jesus Christ has revealed of Father's will in finances for His children.

Radical Commitment to Christ
The New Testament financial paradigm requires embracing a lifestyle that is radically different than the world's lifestyle. It requires a renouncing of ownership. Christ reveals this precisely in a seldom-quoted but powerful and profound verse in Luke's Gospel. He says:

"So therefore, no one of you can be My disciple who does not give up all his own possessions." Luke 14:33

It is noteworthy that there is a *therefore* in this verse. This means that Christ is summing up something He has said previously. In other words, this verse is the sum of the implications of what Christ has said before in this passage. This makes it important to see this verse in its context to understand fully what it means. Here is the context beginning nine verses earlier.

> *Now great multitudes were going along with Him; and He turned and said to them, "If anyone comes to Me, and does not hate his own father and mother and wife and children and brothers and sisters, yes, and even his own life, he cannot be My disciple." Luke 14:25-26*

We can see from this statement, the radical nature of the call to discipleship. Christ is not calling us to hate anyone but Christ is using a very strongly worded comparison. He is saying that in comparison to our commitment and love for Him, our commitment and love for family members must pale in comparison to the point of seeming like hating them. If we are to be His disciple, no commitment to someone or something else can be allowed to compete with our commitment to Him. Christ's next statement continues His encouragement to a radical commitment.

> *"Whoever does not carry his own cross and come after Me cannot be My disciple." Luke 14:27*

A cross to the First Century hearers of Christ's word was not a religious article. It was an ongoing form of execution, a very present symbol of death. Christ was calling them and us to a sacrificial Christ-like lifestyle. He called them and us to take up our own crosses and follow Him to a similar death.

Calculating the Cost

This commitment to living in the world in a radical Christ-like way would be the only way that they could do the work of God. Christ reminds them of this fact in the next three verses by saying:

> *"For which one of you, when he wants to build a tower, does not first sit down and calculate the cost, to see if he had enough to complete it? Otherwise, when he has laid a foundation, and is not able to finish, all who observe it begin to ridicule him, saying, 'This man began to build and was not able to finish.'"*
> *Luke 14:28-30*

What then is the cost of truly following Christ? Everything that we are and all that we have will surely be the cost. Losing a life that we cannot save or leaving wealth that we cannot truly possess is a very small cost to build something of enduring, eternal value. Christ reveals in the next verses that counting this cost also pertains to spiritual warfare. He says:

> *"Or what king, when he sets out to meet another king in battle, will not first sit down and take counsel whether he is strong enough with ten thousand men to encounter the one coming against him with twenty thousand. Or else, while the other is still far away, he sends a delegation and asks terms of peace." Luke 14:31-32*

It is clear that we will not be successful in spiritual warfare if we fail to count the cost of living sacrificially in this world. If we love our lives unto the death, then we will not overcome the devil, his dark angels or his wicked human servants. Now into this context, Christ makes the statement that we began with. He says:

"So therefore, no one of you can be My disciple who does not give up all his own possessions." Luke 14:33

We will not be successful in building anything for Christ that remains or be victorious in spiritual warfare if we fail to heed the radical nature of our call. We cannot live like the world lives. Our foundation must be built securely. We must love Christ supremely and passionately above all other things. We must *hate* all that competes with love for Christ. We must embrace the call to a lifestyle and lifetime of sacrificial commitment. Habitually giving ten-percent of our income and giving other offerings is not a substitute for radical obedience to the real Owner. We must renounce ownership of all wealth and property. We must become obedient stewards. If we fail to embrace these truths and fail to do these things, then Christ's warning in the next verses will apply to us. He says:

"Therefore, salt is good; but if even salt has become tasteless, with what will it be seasoned? It is useless either for the soil or for the manure pile; it is thrown out. He who has ears to hear, let him hear."
Luke 14:34-35

Without this kind of commitment, our works for Christ will be shallow, temporary and useless. We will be salt without taste. We will be useful for nothing. Stewardship is an essential component in building a life and ministry that glorifies Christ. Stewardship is a fundamental and necessary component for successful spiritual warfare.

Christ Does Not Call Impulsive Stewards

Before we motivate a few readers to impulsively give everything away, we must remind all readers that all wealth and property belong to Christ. The Owner alone has the right to tell us to give it to someone else. In other words, a steward that gives everything away better be sure that he is doing it in obedience to the command of the Divine Owner and for no other reason. Father always rewards obedience to the commands of Christ. However, stupidity, impulsiveness and fanaticism are never rewarded. Christians that foolishly give away everything without Christ's command are bad stewards and will not experience divine promotion and supernatural abundance.

We will have much more to discover about New Testament finances in this series of books. We recommend that the reader study the whole series of books on New Testament finances before deciding to do anything with the resources that God has given them. A little knowledge can be a dangerous thing and can produce a heart full of regret. The whole counsel of Christ and His apostles, revealed in the New Testament, is needed before doing anything. Therefore, patience, reflection, prayer and continued study are recommended over action at this time.

~3~

The Rich Young Ruler

The Lord Jesus encountered a man, described in Matthew's, Mark's and Luke's Gospels as being rich, young and a ruler.[1] Some have dismissed what Christ said to this man as not really applying to them because he was rich and they are not rich. However, when the passage is carefully examined, it is clear that Christ's commands to this man regarding money was very similar to His commands to His other disciples. Indeed, Peter saw the similarity and asked Christ about it.

Three Important Questions

The rich young ruler asked Christ three important questions about his lack of assurance about obtaining eternal life. It is clear that he was dissatisfied with his religious experience and was seeking more.

---

[1] This information about this man is gleaned from the three accounts about this man in Matthew, Mark and Luke. No one account has all three characteristics, rich, young and ruler. But all three characteristics appear in the three gospels.

And behold, one came to Him and said, "Teacher, what good thing shall I do that I may obtain eternal life?" And He said to him, "Why are you asking Me about what is good? There is only One who is good; but if you wish to enter into life, keep the commandments." Matthew 19:16-17

The rich young ruler asked Christ about what *good thing* he must *do* to *obtain* eternal life.

Christ Responds to the First Question

Here Christ points the rich young ruler away from doing good things to the fact that God is good. Implicitly, Christ tells this young man that the issue is not his good works but his faith in God. Christ also changes the man's focus from *obtaining* eternal life to *entering into life*. In this Christ reveals to the rich young ruler that he cannot own or possess eternal life since it belongs to God. He can only *enter into life* by relationship to God. Eternal life is not a thing to be obtained but a relationship to the One who is the life, abundant life and eternal life. (Christ will reveal more to the rich young ruler about *entering* later in this passage.) Christ also changes this man's focus from something happening later at his death into something happening *now* in the present while he is still living. Christ continues the conversation with him by telling him that he must keep the commandments in the Law of Moses to enter into life. This is not unexpected since the young man is a Jew and is under the Law.

Christ Responds to the Second Question
The rich young ruler then asks Christ a second reasonable question.

> *He said to Him, "Which ones?" And Jesus said, "YOU SHALL NOT COMMIT MURDER; YOU SHALL NOT COMMIT ADULTERY; YOU SHALL NOT STEAL; YOU SHALL NOT BEAR FALSE WITNESS; HONOR YOUR FATHER AND MOTHER; and YOU SHALL LOVE YOUR NEIGHBOR AS YOURSELF. "*
> *Matthew 19:18-19*

The rich young ruler asks another pertinent question. Since there are hundreds of commandments in the Law of Moses, *which ones should he keep?* Of course, this is the problem with the Law of Moses, you must select some laws to keep and others to ignore or remain ignorant of. There is no way to perfectly keep the Law of Moses all the time. Christ focuses the rich young ruler on six of the ten laws that have been called the *Ten Commandments*. These six are commandments that deal with relationship with man only[2]. The other four deal with the relationship with God. Christ does not mention these other four commandments for a reason. *This is important.* As any educated Jew at that time, the rich young ruler would have been acutely aware that Christ left out the four commandments dealing with

---

[2] We need to note that Christ modified one of these commandments. "Love your neighbor as yourself" seems to be replacing "Do not covet...". Christ might have been hinting and pointing to the other point that is tied to "loving your neighbor as yourself"... the point "You shall love the Lord your God with all your heart, mind, soul and strength." This would certainly match what Christ was about to tell him. His problem is his relationship with money. He cannot love money and God at the same time.

God. Christ is again focusing the young man on his relationship with God. When he asks the third question, the rich young ruler would anticipate that the answer would have something to do with his relationship with God and the four commandments that Christ has purposely left out.

Christ Responds to the Third Question
The rich young ruler asks Christ his third question:

> *The young man said to Him, "All these things I have kept; what am I still lacking?" Matthew 19:20*

Keeping the Law of Moses has not liberated this man. In fact, the Law has revealed to him that something is lacking. He has no life with God. Christ has set the stage for the man to hear what God requires for him to enter into life. Christ could have quoted the other four commandments to him… *You shall have no other God before Me…You shall not make an image…You shall not take the name of the LORD in vain…remember the Sabbath day…* These commandments had to be in this young man's mind. Christ boils it all down for him and reveals his secret gods… those that violate the spirit of the commandment *You shall have no other God before Me…*

The Final Instructions to the Rich Young Ruler
Finally, Christ gives the rich young ruler the real answer to his spiritual dissatisfaction. Christ says:

> *Jesus said to him, "If you wish to be complete, go and sell your possessions and give to the poor, and you*

24

shall have treasure in heaven; and come, follow Me."
Matthew 19:21

Christ tells him if he wants to find what is truly lacking, to be *complete* in his relationship with God and *enter into life* then he must do three things. First, he must *sell all* his possessions. Secondly, he must give the money obtained by selling them to the poor and thirdly, he must follow Christ. It is noteworthy that Christ does not tell him to just give everything away which would have been a reasonably quick and simple process. Instead Christ gives him a longer process to go through; a process that will require him to die each time he sells something for the sake of his relationship with God. His attachments to his material gods will die one by one. This process will liberate him from the power that money and physical possessions have over him. He will be able to become Christ's disciple and wholeheartedly follow Him without hindrance. The rich young ruler will become a true servant and steward of Christ if he *sells all*. However, he does not respond favorably to Christ's instruction.

But when the young man heard this statement, he went away grieved; for he was one who owned much property. Matthew 19:22

The rich young ruler is unable to enter life because of emotional attachment to temporal things. Money is his real god and he is enslaved by it.

Hard for a Rich Man to Enter the Kingdom
The rich young ruler was unwilling to *sell all* to follow
Christ. He was unable to embrace stewardship and entrust
his future to Christ. He would continue to put his trust in
his wealth and continue to know that something was truly
lacking and incomplete in his life. Christ commented to
His disciples on the problem that this young man was
experiencing and how the difficulty has a general
application to anyone with an abundance of financial
resources.

> *And Jesus said to His disciples, "Truly I say to you, it is*
> *hard for a rich man to enter the kingdom of heaven.*
> *"And again I say to you, it is easier for a camel to go*
> *through the eye of a needle, than for a rich man to*
> *enter the kingdom of God." Matthew 19:23-24*

Christ tells us that rich people have a difficult time with
entering the kingdom of Heaven...entering the kingdom of
God and earlier in the passage, *entering life.* It doesn't
require much study to determine that these terms, *kingdom*
of Heaven and *kingdom of God* are interchangeable in the
Gospels and are not describing going to Heaven when we
die. These terms are describing something happening right
now on planet Earth. In this passage, these terms are
describing *entering* the rule of Christ the King over us in
the arena of finances.

Camel through the Eye of a Needle

Christ uses an idiom[3] or an ancient proverb to describe the difficulty of this rich young ruler and rich people in general. He said it was *easier for a camel to go through the eye of a needle than a rich man to enter into the kingdom of God.* There is an ongoing debate among Bible scholars about this idiom's precise meaning. One interpretation simply relates the absolute impossibility of such a task. This interpretation does fit Christ's statement of human impossibility later in this passage. A literal camel simply will not go through a literal eye of a needle. There is a more elaborate and interesting interpretation that focuses on the meaning of the phrase *eye of a needle.* Those who hold this interpretation suggest that historically the eye of a needle was a small gate into a ancient walled city. This gate was smaller than the height of a camel and narrower than a loaded camel would be. The thought here is that a camel must be unloaded of all its goods before attempting to get it through the gate. This would relate to a rich man needing to give away everything in order to be ruled by Christ. Additionally, the camel must be placed on its knees and forcibly pushed and pulled through the gate. The kneeling of the camel would relate to the humility needed for a rich man to fully experience the rule of Christ. Whichever interpretation is correct, the point is that rich persons will have additional obstacles to overcome to become Christ's stewards.

---

[3] Idioms are common in many cultures. For instance, we might say "It is raining cats and dogs." This would be nonsensical to people outside our culture. Its meaning would not be clear.

It is clear that the majority of those who live in the United States of America, Canada and some parts of Europe are indeed rich by Third World's standards. Materialistic gods do compete with Christ in the lives of many Christians whether they consider themselves rich, middle class or poor. The love of money is not restricted to the rich.

No Qualifying Christ's Command

Some want to qualify Christ's commands in this passage to the rich only or to those rich persons who have made money their god. Clearly, financial gods, invoked by greed and fear over money, know no class distinctions. Some of the poor do worship money as well and are just as greedy and fearful about it as some rich people may be. However, if anyone, poor or rich, truly wants to be Christ's steward, they had better be prepared always to *sell all* on His clear and proven command.

The issue of being able to *sell all* is fundamental to be Christ's steward. If we cannot pass this test, then we will never really experience fully what Christ intends for us in the arena of finance. When one has few resources or even is in debt, it is generally easier to embrace the concept of stewardship as a lifestyle. When one has greater resources, it is generally harder to embrace stewardship in the beginning, but the need is just as great. However, sometimes poor people will not give all and embrace stewardship and rich people joyfully embrace the test and will freely give all on command of Christ. No one can precisely predict how individual rich or poor persons might react to the call to stewardship. However, rich people as a group do seem to have a much harder time with selling all.

The Disciples React to Christ's Teaching
Christ's disciples react strongly to the truth revealed by the idiom in this way:

> *And when the disciples heard this, they were very astonished and said, "Then who can be saved?" And looking upon them Jesus said to them, "With men this is impossible, but with God all things are possible." Matthew 19:25-26*

The reason that the disciples are astonished is that Christ was contradicting a common but incorrect belief of first century Jewish culture.[4] They believed that rich men must be righteous or God would not bless them with riches.

Many believed in Christ's day that if a person had wealth it meant that God was rewarding them for being righteous. Christ is saying otherwise. Christ is teaching that this man's love of wealth is an obstacle to pleasing God. Christ is teaching them that this man needs to give away his wealth to please God. This was a shocking revelation to them and prompted the surprised question *Then who can be saved?* The question indicates their utter amazement at the idea that a rich person doesn't have an advantage with God. Christ's answer indicates that no man can cause people, rich or poor, to enter into the kingdom. Only God can do the impossible. Human wisdom and effort cannot convince a rich man or woman into becoming Christ's steward. It must be a work of the Holy Spirit.

---

[4] The New Bible Commentary Revised, pg. 841.

Peter's Important and Revealing Question
Christ's answer prompts another pertinent question, this time from Peter.

> *Then Peter answered and said to Him, "Behold, we have left everything and followed You; what then will there be for us?" Matthew 19:27*

Peter sees the implications of what Christ is saying. He immediately makes a direct connection with what Christ has told the rich young ruler to do with what he and the other eleven disciples have already done. The rich young ruler was given instructions by Christ to *sell all*, give to the poor and to follow Him. The rich young ruler was going to have to leave all his wealth behind to follow Christ. Likewise, the disciples have *left everything* to follow Christ. The rich young ruler was unable to trust Christ with his financial future. In contrast, the disciples entrusted their financial futures and families to Christ. Peter's question now asks what will be the outcome of his and the other eleven disciples' sacrificial commitment to follow Christ.

Christ Promises Glory and Financial Abundance
Christ gives Peter and the disciples a very direct and precise answer. It comes in the form of several promises and predictions about their futures.

> *And Jesus said to them, "Truly I say to you, that you who have followed Me, in the regeneration when the Son of Man will sit on His glorious throne, you also shall sit upon twelve thrones, judging the twelve tribes of Israel." Matthew 19:28*

Christ begins his explanation of the outcome of *leaving everything* and following Him with a focus on the age to come, *the regeneration*. In other words, Christ is saying that the disciples will not experience the full impact of the rewards of following Christ until the age to come dawns. In that age, the disciples will have an important position and function because they *left everything* to follow Christ. When Christ is openly exalted in that age, they too will be exalted with Him. In His next statement Christ agrees with Peter that they have indeed *left everything* behind. Christ also makes an important additional promise that can apply to all believers who meet its conditions.

> *"and everyone who has left houses or brothers or sisters or father or mother or children or farms for My name's sake, shall receive many times as much, and shall inherit eternal life."* Matthew 19:29

What had the disciples *left*? Here Christ describes their commitment to Him. They had *left* behind *houses, brothers, sisters, father, mothers, children[5], and farms*. They had *left behind* the resources of family and property. They had indeed made a financial sacrifice to follow Christ. They had passed the test of stewardship when they wholeheartedly followed Christ and left behind their livelihoods and resources. Christ was asking no less or more of the rich young ruler.

---

[5] We note that no wives were left behind. Because of this, it stands to reason that no small children were left behind either. Christ statement here must mean only grown children. There are several Greek words that mean exclusively small children. They are not used here. However, the Greek word "teknon" that is used here doesn't reveal age at all, only relationship.

A Universal Promise to All
It is important to note the word *everyone* in Christ's statement to Peter. Using the word *everyone* makes it a potentially a universal promise to *every* believer. Not only have the disciples left everything, but also *everyone* who *leaves everything behind* for the sake of Christ will be a partaker of the promise in this verse. Christ extends the promise beyond the disciples, beyond the rich young ruler to us now. Of course, the conditions of this promise are *actually* leaving behind everything, not just being willing to do so. Therefore, being willing is not the test of stewardship. It wasn't enough for the rich young ruler or the disciples to be willing to do this. They *actually* had to do it. The disciples had *actually* left everything behind to follow Christ and He was telling the rich young ruler to actually give everything away. No one has ever passed this test without actually doing it. However, no one has ever given everything away without first being willing to do so.

Many Times as Much in this Age
Christ tells them that they will *receive many times as much* of that which they have left. Matthew's statement here does not say *when* they would *receive many times as much* and therefore, it can be debated that Christ meant that they *would receive many times as much* in the age to come and not in the present age. However, this is not a correct interpretation. When we carefully compare Matthew's version of this story with Mark and Luke's versions, we discover that Christ is speaking of this present age and not the age to come in this second part of His promise. For instance, Mark writes:

32

Jesus said, "Truly I say to you, there is no one who has left house or brothers or sisters or mother or father or children or farms, for My sake and for the gospel's sake, but that he shall receive a hundred times as much now in the present age, houses and brothers and sisters and mothers and children and farms, along with persecutions; and in the age to come, eternal life.
Mark 10:29-30

Mark's Gospel has a few more details about this promise than Matthew's Gospel does. Mark tells us that Christ said that someone who follows Christ would *receive a hundred times as much* as they left. Christ says that they would receive it now in *the present age* and *persecutions* as well. This allows us to conclusively state that Matthew's account was also about this *present age* that we are living in since *no persecutions* will occur in the age to come.

Quoting this verse and claiming a hundred-fold multiplication of financial giving is certainly taking the verse improperly out of its context. Giving does not fulfill the conditions for this promise. Only *leaving all* for the right reasons fulfills the conditions of this promise.

The Importance of Motivation
The minor differences in the three Gospel accounts of the rich young ruler reveal a wealth of interesting information. Mark's Gospel adds the detail of Christ saying that they left behind everything for *My name's sake* and *the gospel's sake.* Luke's Gospel says they left *for the sake of the Kingdom of God.* All these statements point to motivation. You cannot leave everything behind, or sell all, for the

sake of gaining wealth, position or prestige. God does give these things, supernaturally and in abundance. However, God gives these things only as the fruit of godly motivation. They are given to those not seeking them directly but rather to those seeking to love people and to please Christ. They are given to those who only want to faithfully love God and follow Christ. They cannot be sought and obtained in a direct way from God for their own sake. The apostle Paul understood this and wrote:

And if I give all my possessions to feed the poor, and if I deliver my body to be burned, but do not have love, it profits me nothing. 1 Corinthians 13:3

Giving all or leaving all for the wrong reasons will profit you nothing. You will not be a true steward if you fail to root out selfish motivation. Keeping an eternal rather than a temporal perspective on the matter of money is fundamental to having a proper motivation. Christ said:

If anyone wishes to come after Me, let him deny himself, and take up his cross, and follow Me. For whoever wishes to save his life shall lose it; but whoever loses his life for My sake and the gospel's shall save it. For what does it profit a man to gain the whole world, and forfeit his soul? For what shall a man give in exchange for his soul? Mark 8:34b-37

If we wish to follow Christ, we must live as He lived. We must take His instruction on money and possessions to heart. We must lose our lives in this world for His sake and the Gospel. If we walk in this way, we will find abundant life in Him. If we seek to save our lives in the world, we will surely lose them eternally. There is nothing materially worth sacrificing our lives for. Christ Himself is the pearl of great price. He is the treasure hidden in the field. He alone is worth selling all, leaving all and giving all.

The embracing of true stewardship is proven by willingness to sell all, leave all, and give all at the command of Christ. Anyone seeking to be true steward will be tested in certain seasons by such commands. A true steward will joyfully pass each test and discover that the true owner, Christ, will supernaturally promote him by giving him more to care for in subsequent seasons.

Protection from False Ministry

There are those who would abuse and twist the message of stewardship for their own personal financial benefit or even for the benefit of their Christian organization. In fact, the institutional church presently contains many such unethical and shortsighted persons. For those who fear that the message of this book will be abused, we offer the insight that Christ did *not* tell the rich young ruler or His disciples to give to His ministry. The disciples had to *leave all* to follow Christ. The rich young ruler had to sell all and give to the poor *not* to Christ. The disciples did *not* provide Christ with their wealth as part of their commitment to follow Him. The true and faithful servants and stewards of Christ do *not* need money obtained by manipulation, deception or any other unethical means. Abundant financing through Father's supernatural intervention always follows true stewardship. Where Christ guides His servants, He provides for His servants.

Conclusion

The commands to *give all, leave all,* and to *sell all* are not given to a special few of Christ's followers. These commands are for all who wish to be true disciples of Christ. We must give up our possessions if we are truly to follow Christ. All three accounts of the rich young ruler, found in Matthew, Mark and Luke, promise *eternal life* after an earthly life of receiving multiplied blessings from God. This promise, of course, is for those who willingly left *everything behind* for the sake of Christ. Christ then tells us this:

> But many who are first will be last; and the last, first.
> Matthew 19:30

Christ says that the present order of things will be reversed in the future. This statement, although slightly different but meaning the same thing, is repeated at the end of the next chapter of Matthew. Jesus explains its meaning by teaching the parable in the next chapter and then He says it again. The full meaning of this statement and its connection to the rich young ruler is examined in the next chapter of this book.

~4~

Parable of the Vineyard

Many Parables about Money
About half of Christ's parables use money or wealth as a way of illustrating Kingdom truths. Because there are so many of them, the author has chosen to relate a few in this chapter and a few in other chapters where they seem appropriate. The first of these parables in this chapter is a continuation of Christ's teaching just after His meeting with the rich young ruler. It has been called *The Parable of the Vineyard.*

The Parable of the Vineyard
Just after Christ meets the rich young ruler and has His interaction with Peter concerning the eternal and temporal consequences of leaving all to follow Him, Christ makes His statement about the first being last and the last being first. Here Christ begins to explain this statement by telling the disciples a parable.

For the kingdom of heaven is like a landowner who went out early in the morning to hire laborers for his vineyard. And when he had agreed with the laborers for a denarius for the day, he sent them into his vineyard. Matthew 20:1-2

Like many of His parables, Christ is describing the kingdom of Heaven by means of comparison. This parable is not describing the place Heaven but the rule of Heaven or God upon the Earth.[1] Christ presents Himself in this parable as a landowner with a vineyard. He presents believers as the workers being hired throughout the parable.

The First Four Groups of Workers
The landowner hires the first group of workers early in the day. They agree with the landowner for a fair wage; a denarius for a full day's labor and they go into the vineyard to work early in the day. Then the second, third, and fourth group are hired. Christ says:

And he went out about the third hour and saw others standing idle in the market place; and to those he said, "You too go into the vineyard, and whatever is right I will give you." And so they went. Again he went out about the sixth and the ninth hour, and did the same thing. Matthew 20:3-5

Three more groups of workers are hired and sent by the landowner into the vineyard to work. The landowner saw that they were *idle*, doing nothing, and he gave them purpose. The difference between the first group of laborers and these three groups of laborers is that the landowner did not agree with them for a precise wage. He simply

---

[1] Matthew often substitutes the word *Heaven* for *God* in these parables.

promised them that he would give them *whatever is right*. A strong element of trust is involved in these three later transactions with the landowner that does not exist with the first transaction. The workers must believe that the landowner will be fair with them in order to begin to work in the vineyard. Of course, each group selected later in the day would put in less labor simply because there would be less time to do it before the end of the day.

The Fifth and Final Group of Workers

Christ continues the parable by telling us about the last group hired. He says:

> *And about the eleventh hour he went out, and found others standing; and he said to them, "Why have you been standing here idle all day long?" They said to him, 'Because no one hired us." He said to them, "You too go into the vineyard." Matthew 20:6-7*

The last group is without purpose or labor for nearly the entire day. This final group is sent into the vineyard by the landowner at the end of the day. The landowner doesn't even give them the same assurance that he will be fair to them. For them to respond requires even greater trust. Yet they risk little in laboring since the day is nearly finished. Only one hour of work time remains before the workday finishes, evening begins and the workers expect wages.

The Payment of Wages

That time arrives for payment of the promised wages in the next verses.

And when evening had come, the owner of the vineyard said to his foreman, "Call the laborers and pay them their wages, beginning with the last group to the first." Matthew 20:8-9

The landowner has his foreman pay the workers in the *reverse order* in which they were hired. He pays those who worked the least amount of time first. This is important. Christ says:

And when those hired about the eleventh hour came, each one received a denarius. And when those hired first came they thought that they would receive more; and they also received each one a denarius. Matthew 20:10

When those who had worked the longest saw that the foreman paid those who worked the least a denarius, they mistakenly thought that they would receive more. They also received a denarius, which is a fair day's wage. It is noteworthy that there would have been no problem if the workers had been paid in the order that they had been hired. The first group of workers would have left after receiving what they had been promised and would have been unaware that the other groups had gotten the same wage. That, however, is the point of the parable. The reaction of this first group is the focus of this parable.

The Reaction of the First Group
Christ told this parable to highlight the reaction of this final group to make an important point. He says:

And when they received it, they grumbled at the landowner, saying, "These last men have worked only one hour, and you have made them equal to us who have borne the burden and the scorching heat of the day." Matthew 20:11-12

Those that worked the longest thought that they should receive more. By using comparison with the other workers as their standard, they felt that they were being treated unfairly.

The Landowner's Reply to the First Group
The landowner then reminded them of the real standard of what was right and wrong. That standard was what they had agreed with him to receive for their labor.

But he answered and said to one of them, "Friend, I am doing you no wrong; did you not agree with me for a denarius?" Matthew 20:13

The real standard was what the workers and the landowner had previously agreed upon. The landowner reminds them of this fact and the fact that he is being faithful to that which he agreed upon. The landowner then tells them to take what is theirs (their wage of a denarius) and to leave. He then asks them two more pertinent questions.

"Take what is yours and go your way, but I wish to give to this last man the same as to you. Is it not lawful for me to do what I wish with what is my own? Or is your eye envious because I am generous?" Matthew 20:14-15

41

The landowner asks these disgruntled workers two important questions. First of all, he asks if he has the right to do whatever he wishes with that which belongs to him. Of course, the answer is that the landowner certainly has the right to do whatever he wishes with that which he owns. Secondly, the landowner asks if they are envious because he is being generous with the other groups. The parable ends with a statement that is similar to the beginning of it. Christ says:

Thus the last shall be first, and the first last.
Matthew 20:16

The meaning of this on the surface is clear. The order of paying these groups was reversed. The last to work were paid first. The first to work were paid last. However, it is clear that there is more to this parable. *What is it?*

The Meaning of the Parable
What is Christ revealing by this parable? Simply this, that there are two approaches to serving Christ. The first approach relates to the *first* group of workers. They are serving for a set wage, a reward for service. They look to their hard work and seek what they deserve from the landowner as a result. These reward seekers envy those who discover the amazing grace of the landowner. Conversely, each of the other four groups in this parable enters into relationship with the landowner and trusts him with the final outcome without mention of a specific reward. What we see here is a comparison of dead, legalistic, reward-of-heaven-driven religion with true stewardship. A true steward trusts that Christ will be more

than just fair in rewards. He looks beyond wages and sees abundant grace and generosity coming out of his relationship with God. He is not a wage earner but a steward. He is not bound by the idea of justice and reward for labor but rather expects that grace of the True Owner will be much greater than justice and reward could ever be. He is bound by love and service not justice and reward. He radically trusts the True Owner.

Like the first group in the parable, the rich young ruler was looking for a precise wage. He was working for the reward of keeping the commandments. He was willing to work even harder for the wage of eternal life but sensed that something important was missing. Christ called him to a higher way, requiring relationship, radical trust and faith in Christ for the outcome. Unfortunately for him, he was unwilling to radically entrust himself to Christ in the same way that Peter and the other disciples had. He was unwilling to *give all, leave all* or *sell all.* Truly, he had good reason to go away grieved. He did not *sell all* and obtain the treasure hidden in the field. He did not *sell all* for the pearl of great price. He did not follow Christ like Peter and the other disciples by leaving all, selling all, and giving all.

Religious Lovers of Money
There were religious people who loved money listening and reacting to Christ as He said these words recorded above. Luke writes:

Now the Pharisees, who were lovers of money, were listening to all these things, and they were scoffing at

Him. And He said to them, "You are those who justify yourselves in the sight of men, but God knows your hearts; for that which is highly esteemed among men is detestable in the sight of God." Luke 16:14-15

They loved money and therefore were unable to receive Christ as their Lord. Money was their savior and lord. They used religious teaching to mask their greed and produced religious reasoning to avoid true stewardship. They made themselves out to be financially righteous for the respect of men but were not right with God at all. Thy cloaked themselves with self-righteousness but their attitudes and behavior involving money were detestable in the sight of God. The true owner, the King of Kings, was not allowed to rule His own property. They were blind to Christ establishing a new way to relate to finances. Christ said to them in the next verse:

"The Law and the Prophets were proclaimed until John; since then the gospel of the kingdom of God is preached and everyone is forcing his way into it." Luke 16:16

Many have taken this verse out of its context and given it general application. While that is not entirely wrong, the context of this verse is very important. This verse is about a believer's relationship with money. Christ has paid the price for our financial blessing. We are no longer debtors to God as were the Children of Israel. The gospel reveals that Christ has *paid in full* the price of our redemption. There has been a radical change from the Old Testament through Christ's death and resurrection. A new way has

44

been established concerning finances. This is a radical change in the nature of things. We must force our way into this realm of abundant finances. We must allow radical trust in Christ to empty our hands of ownership. We must believe that Father will supply His stewards graciously through Christ.

Entering into Christ's kingdom rule requires a forceful, aggressive, seeking faith and a radical trust. Opposition of the flesh, the world, and the devil must be overcome before we experience the benefits of stewardship. Spirits of fear, anxiety and greed must be cast out and the flesh crucified completely. Faith and trust in the Divine Owner must arise if supernatural stewardship is to be seen throughout the Earth in the last days.

A Financial Parable Explains the Second Coming

In the twelfth chapter of Luke, there is a great deal of Christ's teaching on finances and stewardship. This is not exactly stated in the form of a parable but has some of the same characteristics since He is explaining a parable that came before. Therefore, it is included in this chapter. Early in Chapter Twelve of Luke, Christ deals with the subject of greed and anxiety. Later in this chapter He focuses on the fact of His second coming to Earth. Christ's second coming has an important relationship to how we should think about money. Christ says:

You too, be ready; for the Son of Man is coming at an hour that you do not expect. Luke 12:40

In the parable just before this verse, Christ compares His coming to a thief breaking into a house. He says that we should not be unprepared like those who are taken advantage of by a thief but should be ready for His coming. Peter reacts to Christ's teaching by saying:

> *And Peter said, "Lord are You addressing this parable to us, or to everyone else as well?" And the Lord said, "Who then is the faithful and sensible steward, who his master will put in charge of his servants, to give them their rations at the proper time?" Luke 12:41-42*

Christ answers Peter by directing him back to the truth of stewardship. A steward will be faithful. A steward will be sensible. A steward is in charge of Christ's servants. A steward gives the other servants their rations at the proper time. *Who is this kind of steward?* Everyone who hears and receives the call to be prepared for Christ's Second Coming is this kind of steward. This gives a clear picture of the duties of Christ's stewards. They supply financially the other servants of Christ until He returns. *What about the steward himself?* Christ says:

> *"Blessed is that slave whom his master finds so doing when he comes. Truly I say to you, that he will put him in charge of all his possessions." Luke 12:43-44*

The steward is to continue to provide for the other slaves until Christ comes. If he is found faithfully serving Christ when He comes, he will be promoted. Obviously, if we have been blessed financially, we have responsibility to use what Father has given us to care for Christ's servants.

The Unprepared Steward

However, if he does not continue to serve the other slaves and provide for their needs, his outcome will be different at Christ's return. Christ says in the next verse:

> *But if that slave says in his heart, "My master will be a long time in coming," and begins to beat the slaves, both men and women, and to eat and drink and get drunk; the master of that slave will come on a day when he does not expect him, and at an hour he does not know, and will cut him in pieces, and assign him a place with the unbelievers. Luke 12:45-46*

This steward is no longer living as if his Master will return. He has forgotten his duties to care for the other servants in the household. He abuses those who he was supposed to care for. He lives as if the wealth of the master was his to do with as he chooses. He lives a consumptive, lavish lifestyle with the means that was supposed to be used to care for the other servants. That steward is promised an unwelcome surprise. Christ's coming (or his own death) will be unexpected and he will be severely judged for his abuse of the other servants when he was commanded to care for them. He will be treated as he treated others. He will be treated as if he were not part of Christ's household.

Stewardship Principles of Judgment

Christ continues this discourse with specifics about the final outcome of unfaithful stewards who were not as abusive as the one described above.

And that slave who knew his master's will and did not get ready or act in accord with his will, shall receive many lashes... Luke 12:47

Here is a steward who was knew the Master's will and yet ignored it. He did not prepare for Christ's coming or take good care of Christ's other servants. He will be severely punished but not finally judged as if he were lost. He will be saved even if all his works and rewards are burned up. However, the issue is knowledge of the will of God and God's commitment of resources to the steward. Christ then says:

...but the one who did not know it, and committed deeds worthy of a flogging, will receive but few. And from everyone who has been given much shall much be required; and to whom they entrusted much, of him they will ask all the more. Luke 12:48

A poor steward who was not entirely aware that he was being a poor steward will also be punished. However, his punishment will be much less severe than the steward that understood clearly what his Master wanted and ignored it because he believed the accounting was not coming quickly. The revelation and commitment to stewardship releases gracious amounts of resources. The greater the resources available to the steward create greater accountability to the Master. No one should ever forget this or act as if a reckoning with the Master is not coming.

48

Common Elements in Many Parables

It is worthwhile to expend a moment to review the five common elements in these parables. Christ often repeats these five elements and so it is clear that we should be aware of them.

- The owner gives resources to his servants or stewards.
- The owner goes away for an unspecified time.
- The servants or stewards must function in the owner's financial interest in his absence and increase His holdings.
- The owner returns and makes the stewards account for what they did with his resources when he was gone.
- The faithful stewards are rewarded and promoted and the unfaithful stewards are punished and discharged from service.

Of course, Christ is the owner and we must function as good stewards and increase His holdings until He returns. The next financial parable is outlined in the next chapter. It has all these common elements and much more.

~5~

Parable of the Ten Minas

The Parable of the Ten Minas

This parable begins with an explanation of why Christ told it. He told it because He was near Jerusalem and many in the audience thought that He was going to become the King of Israel and overthrow the Roman military occupation when He entered Jerusalem. The text says:

And while they were listening to these things, He went on to tell a parable, because He was near Jerusalem, and they supposed that the kingdom of God was going to appear immediately. Luke 19:11

Christ used this parable to help them understand that His kingdom was not going to appear immediately. Christ is presented as a nobleman in this parable. The nobleman is leaving to receive a kingdom and then to return.

He said therefore, "A certain nobleman went to a distant country to receive a kingdom for himself, and then return." Luke 19:12

This is, of course, a description of Christ. Christ has left the Earth to receive His kingdom and will return to Earth on the Father's specified day. The nobleman in the parable before leaving to receive the kingdom calls his slaves:

> *And he called ten of his slaves, and gave them ten minas, and said to them, "Do business with this until I come back." Luke 19:13*

The nobleman distributes ten minas to ten of his slaves and gives them specific instructions.

The term *mina* is a Semitic word that means both a weight and a sum of money in ancient Greece, Egypt and Israel. It was worth 100 shekels or 100 drachmas or one-sixtieth of a talent. It represented 100 days wages. In weight, it is about 15 ounces and represents about $20 total today but would have a much greater purchasing power when Christ told this parable.

The nobleman tells his slaves to *do business* with the minas until he comes. The phrase *do business* is a translation of the Greek *pragmateueomai*. This word means *to accomplish by economic traffic* or *to gain by trading*. The English adjective *pragmatic* comes from the first part of this verb. The first part of the word, the Greek noun *pragma* means *business*. The nobleman was telling them to be active in business with these assets and to increase them by trading while he was gone.

While very few Christians doubt that Christ intends for us to increase spiritually, many Christians do not see the need to increase materially. Many are very passive concerning money and are not obeying the Master's words here with the assets that He has given them. Christ has gone to receive His kingdom and while He is gone, we should be doing business for Him with the financial assets that He has given. Fear and greed do not motivate the true Christian steward but rather the desire to please the Lord and increase His kingdom on Earth in everyway. Stewards should seek a mighty increase through business in order to finance kingdom works and to be generous in every way.

Archelaus, Caesar and the Jews
The passage continues with an unusual element in the story. Christ says:

> *But his citizens hated him, and sent a delegation after him, saying, "We do not want this man to reign over us." Luke 19:14*

Christ was peaking the interest of His hearers by referring to a well-known situation. In 4 BC, Archelaus, the son of Herod the Great went to Rome to have his royal power confirmed over Israel but a delegation of prominent Jews came with a protest against him. They said to Caesar *we do not want this man to reign over us.* As a result, Augustus Caesar severely limited Archelaus' powers. The attitude revealed by this incident is representative of the negative reaction of many people toward the claim of Christ as King over them.

The Return of the Nobleman and the Accounting

In the parable, the nobleman now returns after receiving the kingdom. This means, of course, that the nobleman is now a king. Christ says in the next verse:

And it came about that when he returned, after receiving the kingdom, he ordered that these slaves, to whom he had given the money, be called to him in order that he might know what business they had done.
Luke 19:15

He calls the slaves that he had given the money. The word *money* is translated from the Greek word *argurion* meaning *silver*. He wanted to know what the slaves had done with his silver in trading for increase.

The First Slave's Accounting

The various slaves begin giving reports of their success in trading to the nobleman.

And the first appeared, saying, "Master, your mina has made ten minas more." And he said to him, "Well done, good slave, because you have been faithful in a very little thing, be in authority over ten cities."
Luke 19:16-17

The first slave has been dramatically successful. He has increased the nobleman's mina by a factor of ten. Because this slave has been faithful in this small matter of money, he is given authority over ten cities in the nobleman's kingdom that he has just recently received. The increase of money has a direct relationship to the authority that this slave is given in the nobleman's kingdom. A factor of ten increase in money means authority over ten cities. This is a principle of promotion stated by Christ in the Parable of the Unrighteous Steward as well[1]. Faithfulness in a small matter of finances means promotion and authority in larger matters.

The Second Slave's Accounting
The second slave makes his report to the nobleman.

> *And the second came, saying, "Your mina, master, has made five minas." And he said to him also, "And you are to be over five cities." Luke 19:18-19*

The reaction of the nobleman is similar. According to the success of the slave in multiplying the mina in trading, authority over cities is given. A factor of five in multiplying the money means authority over five cities. The nobleman is completely consistent and principled in the way that he rewards these two slaves.

The Third Slave's Accounting
The third slave appears and has a different kind of report.

> *And another came, saying, "Master, behold your mina, which I kept put away in a handkerchief; for I was afraid of you, because you are an exacting man; you take up what you did not lay down, and reap what you did not sow." Luke 19:20-21*

[1] See Luke 16:10-11

This slave did not do as the nobleman instructed. He failed to trade with the financial resources that he had been given. Instead the hid the money to return it intact to the nobleman.

The reason that he did not obey the nobleman is that he was afraid of him. He was afraid of the nobleman because he had an inaccurate and negative view of him. The slave said that the nobleman was an *exacting* man. This is the Greek word *austeros*. This word comes from a root word meaning literally *to be dry*. The English word *austere* comes from it. It means that which is disagreeable because it is not matured by age like unripe fruit. In application, this word means *harsh* and *severe.*

Beyond this negative characterization of the nobleman, the slave also has an accusation. He accuses the nobleman of *taking up where he has not laid down and reaping where he has not sowed.* This accusation against his master is that the master was unjustly appropriating the increase of other men's labors. This slave apparently did not know how the master, the nobleman, intended to reward him for his labor. He did not trust the nobleman and therefore sought to avoid punishment by incurring a loss in investment. So he put away the mina to return to the master.

The Nobleman's Judgment of the Third Slave
There are interesting elements in the reaction of the nobleman to this particular slave. The nobleman says to the third slave…

He said to him, "By your own words I will judge you, you worthless slave. Did you know that I am an exacting man, taking up what I did not lay down, and reaping what I did not sow? Then why did you not put the money in the bank, and having come, I would have collected it with interest?" Luke 19:22-23

The slave got just what he was expecting. He expected a harsh reaction and received one. He was judged by his own words. The third slave was rebuked for not even entrusting the banker with the money so that he could have drawn interest. This is an extremely interesting comment by Christ in this parable. Christ sees drawing interest on money as kind of a *minimum* thing that someone that is fearful should do. It is not really what he expects for His faithful and believing servants. He expects them to invest and do business with what He gives and come back with a *multiplication of the principle* not just interest. This also speaks to initiative. Financial passivity will not produce what Christ wishes. It is a reflection of fearfulness not faith. Christ expects us to actively invest and have a multiplication of the resources that He gives us.

Christ, through the words of the nobleman, describes the third slave as *worthless* in this verse. This is the Greek word *poneros*. It is often translated *wicked*. Why was the man *wicked*? He had a wrong view of the nobleman that made him fearful and produced disobedience to his commands and that made him unproductive. Many people ong view of God that makes them fearful . They do not come to Christ as Savior o not see God properly. They are full of accusations against God and think of Him being harsh. They also unfortunately may be judged by their own words and attitudes toward God rather than experiencing the mercy and grace of God in Jesus Christ.

This parable is also found in Matthew's Gospel in Chapter 25 with a couple of small differences that are interesting. The Gospel of Matthew adds another word to the description of the third slave in this parable in verse 26. It says *you wicked, lazy slave*. Matthew adds the word *lazy*. This is the Greek word *okneros*. It means *one who shirks his duty or is lazy or slothful*. The nobleman sees the third slave as one who failed to do his duty because he was lazy.

The Principle of Spiritual Momentum
The nobleman then has the third slave's mina taken away from him.

> *And he said to the bystanders, "Take the mina away from him, and give it to the one who has the ten minas." And they said to him, "Master, he has ten minas already." Luke 19:24-25*

The nobleman tells the bystanders to give the mina to the one who has ten. The bystanders react to this development. They say that that the first slave has ten minas already. The nobleman then relates a principle, a truth that explains why he is giving the mina to the one who has ten. He says:

> *I tell you, that to everyone who has shall more be given, but from the one who does not have, even what he does have shall be taken away. Luke 19:26*

This is the profound truth of *spiritual momentum.* Momentum is the strength or force moving an object that keeps growing as additional force is added. Christ always rewards fruitfulness with additional resources. These resources may be natural and spiritual. Natural resources may be given in the form of assisting people and money. Christ may give additional spiritual capacity in the form of revelation and power to help people. Christ causes resources to be added to that which is moving for Him. This increases the momentum of that which is already fruitful and makes it exceedingly fruitful.

Fruitfulness is always produced by Christ-centerness and enduring diligence in the revealed will of God. For that which is not moving, not being fruitful for Christ, He takes away resources and gives those resources to that which is moving and being fruitful. This is the truth of *spiritual inertia.* Those who fail to use and multiply the resources that God gives will eventually lose those resources. God will give them to someone with spiritual momentum. This is the great wisdom of God. *Why give resources to that which is not fruitful?* It makes a great deal of sense to give more resources to the one who is producing greater and greater amounts of fruit.

The Other Seven Slaves

Christ, through the nobleman in this parable, then says:

> *But these enemies of mine, who did not want me to reign over them, bring them here and slay them in my presence. Luke 19:27*

Since this parable began with ten slaves, these enemies must be the other seven slaves. The nobleman gave ten minas to ten slaves. Two accounted for themselves well. The third accounted poorly and seven did not account at all. These failed to acknowledge that they had a responsibility to account to the nobleman. They must have forgotten their stewardship and took the mina for themselves. They must have thought that the nobleman would not return. This danger exists for us all. To focus on the temporal rather than the eternal is a basic temptation and spiritual danger to every believer. A day of accounting awaits us all. Let us account for our stewardships well on that day.

The next chapter has a powerful parable that contains some similar truths as the Parable of the Ten Minas and yet has much more to teach us. It is called the Parable of the Unrighteous Steward. This unusual parable reveals much of the surprising Divine purpose for money.

~6~
Parable of the Unrighteous Steward

This next financial parable in our review is perhaps the most difficult of Christ's parables to interpret properly. The parable of the unrighteous steward is about the believer's relationship to wealth. Since this steward is presented as unrighteous and unfaithful, it would seem that we should draw some lessons of what not to do. However, this is not the case. Instead, we are to emulate the *practicality* but not the unrighteousness of the unrighteous steward. Hear the words of Christ:

> *Now He was also saying to the disciples, "There was a certain rich man who had a steward, and this steward was reported to him as squandering his possessions." Luke 16:1*

Someone reports to the owner that the steward is not faithfully executing his duties. The steward is accused of squandering the rich man's possessions. The rich man, the owner, calls for the steward.

And he called him and said to him, "What is this I hear about you? Give an account of your stewardship, for you can no longer be steward." Luke 16:2

The owner asks for an accounting of the stewardship and makes the steward aware that this is a final accounting and he will no longer be the rich man's steward after the accounting. This implies that there is strong evidence of the steward's irresponsibility. The unfaithful steward reacts to this development in this manner.

And the steward said to himself, "What shall I do, since my master is taking the stewardship away from me? I am not strong enough to dig; I am ashamed to beg. I know what I shall do, so that when I am removed from the stewardship, they will receive me into their homes." Luke 16:3-4

The steward apparently knows that the accusation is true and he will be found wanting in the accounting. As a result of this realization, the steward evaluates his options. He determines that he cannot dig because he is not strong enough. Whether or not this is true or he is simply lazy we cannot say from the evidence that the parable presents. He determines cannot beg because is ashamed. This sounds much like pride. Nevertheless, he is unprepared body and soul for losing his stewardship.

The Steward's Unrighteous Solution
The steward determines a third course of action that is clearly unrighteous and damaging to the owner's interests.

And he summoned each one of his master's debtors, and he began saying to the first, "How much do you owe my master?" And he said, "A hundred measures of oil." And he said to him, "Take your bill, and sit down quickly and write fifty." Then he said to another, "And how much do you owe?" And he said, "A hundred measures of wheat." He said to him," Take your bill, and write eighty." Luke 16:5-7

He significantly reduces the debt of each of these two men in order that they will be indebted to the unrighteous steward in the future when he is no longer a steward. He grants them a financial favor that he intends to collect when he needs help. While this is a wrong thing to do, the owner, the master, reacts in a positive fashion to the *shrewdness* of the unrighteous steward.

And his master praised the unrighteous steward because he had acted shrewdly; for the sons of this age are more shrewd in relation to their own kind than the sons of light. Luke 16:8

The word translated *shrewdly* here is the Greek word *phronimos*. It can be translated as *prudent, sensible, practically wise* as well as *shrewd.*[1] In light of this, the unrighteous steward was praised for being *practical* concerning his own situation using the owner's financial resources. Christ then says that the people of this world are more sensible and practical about financial matters when dealing with other worldly people. They use money to make friends of other worldly people. However, they do it

---

[1] See "Wise" Pg. 1234, Vine's Dictionary of New Testament Words

for the wrong reasons. They do it to gain power, prestige, or additional wealth. Believers need to do the same thing with money but for good kingdom reasons.

Make Friends by Means of Money

The unrighteous steward used the situation to make friends out of these two men. That, of course, is exactly the point that Christ is trying to make. He says in the next verse:

> *And I say to you, make friends for yourselves by means of the mammon of unrighteousness; that when it fails, they may receive you into the eternal dwellings.*
> *Luke 16:9*

Here Christ summarizes what the point of the parable is. He is warning us that we should prepare for an inevitable time that will involve the *failure* of money and the end of our stewardships. Therefore, using money to make friends is very wise in light of this coming failure of money. There will be an accounting at the coming of Christ. All our money and wealth will fail us in that day. We prepare for that accounting by using unrighteous mammon to *make friends* that will receive us into *eternal dwellings*. By using the phrase *eternal dwellings*, Christ both points us to the coming time of our own deaths and also to His own return. We are to use money to build relationships with others that are eternal. If we make friends of others for the sake of the kingdom of God using unrighteous mammon, then they will receive us as friends when we die or when Christ returns.

Money should be used to build kingdom, Church and family friendships. The divine purpose of money is not security but is relational. This would include evangelism of the lost as well as existing relationships to other believers. This requires insight into the age to come when an accounting for our earthly stewardship will be given.

General Principles of New Testament Finances

After this point, Christ gives some general principles of finances that correct any thought that he is commending unrighteousness. He says:

> *He who is faithful in a very little thing is faithful also in much; and he who is unrighteous in a very little thing is unrighteous also in much. Luke 16:10*

First, the way that a person takes care of a small amount of resources reveals how he will take care of many resources. This is a common-sense principle of spiritual promotion. A person who takes good care of a small amount of money reveals the capacity to take care of more. A faithful steward would use money to make friends for the kingdom of God. Another principle of promotion is found in the next verse.

> *If therefore you have not been faithful in the use of unrighteous mammon, who will entrust the true riches to you? And if you have not been faithful in the use of that which is another's, who will give you that which is your own? Luke 16:11-12*

Secondly, a person who is a good steward over money for *another*, that is God, will also be a good steward of *true riches*. *What are true riches?* Clearly, Christ is drawing a stark comparison between unrighteous mammon and *something else* that He calls *true riches*. *What is that something else?* The apostle Paul tells us in the book of Colossians what this is. He writes:

> *Christ Himself, in whom are hidden all the treasures of wisdom and knowledge. Colossians 2:2b-3*

It is certain that Christ Himself is the hidden treasure that every believer should seek. Intimate and personal knowledge of Christ Himself is priceless. Christ draws again a stark contrast in the next verse by saying.

> *No servant can serve two masters; for either he will hate the one, and love the other, or else he will hold to one, and despise the other. You cannot serve God and mammon. Luke 16:13*

An intimate relationship with Christ ruling over us is true riches. Either we serve Him or we will serve money. These two opposing rulers are mutually exclusive. Both demand complete consecration. You may only serve one. Unrighteous mammon has a strong corrupting influence on those who seek and are ruled by it. Either we seek the Kingdom and serve Christ as Master and use money to make friends or we will serve money and come to hate and despise the claims of Christ over us.

~7~

Seeking the Kingdom

In a well-known passage of the New Testament often cited as *the Sermon on the Mount,* there is a short portion of Scripture has been called *the Lord's Prayer.* In this teaching on prayer, Christ instructs His disciples to pray about their daily need for food. This prayer is also found in Luke 11:1-4 where it is followed by two short parables that strongly encourage persistence in prayer until an answer comes. This reveals that getting prayers for needs answered requires daily prayer and a militant attitude. Christ says within this prayer found in Matthew's Gospel:

> *Thy kingdom come, they will be done on earth as it is in heaven. Give us this day our daily bread. Matthew 6:10-11*

All believers need to know that God will answer their prayers concerning their basic needs such as food. It is clear that Christ intends them to pray for these matters *daily*. If they fail to experience answered prayer because they failed to pray, then are severe consequences to

Christ's rule in their lives. This failure may be common in a materialistic culture where food is in abundance. It is more than just a coincidence that prayer concerning the daily need for food follows prayer about the kingdom coming and the will of God being done on the earth. The basic needs of food, drink and clothing are discussed in detail a few verses later in this passage. Christ points out that anxiety concerning these material things militate against the believer being ruled by God.

Storing Treasures on Earth

A few verses beyond the Lord's Prayer in the Gospel of Matthew, Christ reveals a great deal about proper attitudes about material things. Christ starts His discourse about storing treasures but will end with discussing needs. Christ says:

> *Do not lay up for yourselves treasures upon earth, where moth and rust destroy, and where thieves break in and steal... Matthew 6:19*

The Greek word for *treasures* is *thesauros*. This word actually describes a place of safekeeping such as a small box, a chest, or a storehouse rather than the valuables themselves. Therefore, it is a general word to describe all kinds of valuables that require safekeeping.

The Two Weaknesses of Treasures

Christ first reveals the two inherent weaknesses of treasures. The first is that *moth and rust destroy* treasures. The Greek word for *moth* describes a moth that destroys clothing. This reminds us that the work of insects and other living things such as rodents can destroy some valuable items such as artwork, clothing, or paper items. Also Christ says that *rust destroys*. The Greek word for *rust* is *brosis*. This word means literally *an eating* and is used metaphorically to denote *rust*. Christ is using this word to describe the fact that insects, animals, direct sunlight, and oxidation that cause rusting destroy valuable things. Valuables do not retain their value without ongoing protection against nature.

Christ adds another phrase about the nature of treasures that reveals the second inherent weakness. He says *where thieves break in and steal.* Beyond the problems of the fragility of valuables is the problem of thieves. Wherever there is something of worldly value, there are people of bad character who would use theft, violence, and murder to obtain it. Wherever protections of valuables exist, there are those who have the wicked ingenuity to discover how to break into that protection and obtain the valuables. The greater the value of a treasure, the greater the motivation to protect it for owners and to obtain it for thieves. In other words, no adequate protection can ever exist for treasures on the earth. They can never really be secure.

Storing Treasures in Heaven
In light of the two problems of protection of valuables, Christ says:

> *But lay up for yourselves treasures in heaven, where neither moth nor rust destroys, and where thieves do not break in or steal... Matthew 6:20*

Christ encourages us not to get involved in the insecurity of trying to secure treasures upon the earth but rather to lay up treasures in heaven. Treasures in heaven are truly secure. Neither nature can damage them or thieves steal them. In this passage, Christ does not tell us what the natures of these treasures are or how to lay them up in these verses. However, He does tell us that these treasures will be secure in heaven because there is nothing to destroy or steal those treasures.

A Truth of the Heart

Christ reveals a specific psychological trait of humanity in His next phase in this passage. This is a universal trait. Christ says this:

> _...for where your treasure is, there will your heart be also. Matthew 6:21_

This is an extremely important truth. Our heart will be where we lay up our treasure. The Greek word for _heart_ is _kardia_. The English word _cardiac_ comes from this Greek word. It means a literal physical heart but also meant in Christ's day the entire mental, emotional, moral and spiritual elements of a person. In this context, this means that the mental, emotional and spiritual focus of a person will be determined by where they lay up their treasures. Therefore, the focus of every person is limited to only two places: _heaven or earth._

The Lamp of the Body is the Eye

Christ elaborates further on this truth of the power of a person's inner focus by saying:

The lamp of the body is the eye; if therefore your eye is clear, your whole body will be full of light.
Matthew 6:22

Whatever the eye focuses upon will create the inner experience of a person. If the eye focuses on heavenly treasures, then that eye is clear and the inner experience of that person will be full of light. The Greek word that is rendered *clear* by translators here is *haplous*. It means *simple* or *single*. It means in this context *singleness of purpose or vision.* When a person has a singleness of vision upon heavenly things, Christ and His Kingdom, then that person will be full of light. Christ explains the alternative as well. He says:

But if your eye is bad, your whole body will be full of darkness. If therefore the light that is in you is darkness, how great is the darkness! Matthew 6:23

If the eye is focused on earthly things, then the eye is *bad*. The Greek word translated *bad* is *poneros*. It means *wicked, worthless* or *bad.* If the focus is on worldly wealth, then the life will be full of darkness. The earthly focus will produce an inner experience of darkness. Greed and anxious fears will rule the inner parts of those who focus on worldly wealth.

Cannot Serve Two Masters
In this passage Christ has told us that there are two competing places to lay up treasures. Christ has told us that there are two competing places to focus our attention. He

has made it clear that it is impossible to lay up treasures in both. He has made it clear that our attention cannot be in two places at the same time. Now He adds two more competing things to this list. He says:

> _No one can serve two masters; for either he will hate the one and love the other, or he will hold to one and despise the other. You cannot serve God and mammon._
> _Matthew 6:24_

Christ adds _masters_ to the list of competing things. The Greek word for _master_ is _kurios._ It is often translated as _lord_ and simply means _one who rules or exercises power._ The word transliterated as _mammon_ comes from _mamonas_ and is a common Aramaic word for _riches._ This word is probably derived from a Hebrew word meaning _steadfast_ or _firm,_ hence that which is to be trusted. Christ has personified _mammon_ in this passage and is using this word as if it were a name of a competing god. Christ is strongly suggesting that wealth is a god that some put their trust in.

Christ tells us that God and mammon have competing and exclusive claims on us. We cannot serve both. We can only serve one. We cannot love both. We can only love one. If we chose one, then we will hate the other. If we hold to one, then we will despise the other. Again, Christ tells us that each will make an exclusive claim to us. We can only choose one place to lay up treasures. We can only focus our attention on one thing. We can only have one master.

Christ's Command About Anxiety
Christ now explains why He forbids being anxious over material needs. He says:

"For this reason I say to you, do not be anxious for your life, as to what you shall eat, or what you shall drink; nor for your body, as to what you shall put on. Is not life more than food, and the body than clothing?"
Matthew 6:25

Christ begins His explanation with the basic needs of food, drink, and clothing. He uses unusual rhetorical questions to guide His hearers to a larger vision of Father's care of His children. He asks if *life* is *more* than food and the *body more* than clothing. There are several Greek words that are translated *life* in the New Testament. In this case, this is the Greek word *psuche*. We draw the English words *psychic* or *psychology* from this Greek word. It is translated in the New Testament with different English words such as *heart, mind, soul, life* or other English words. In this context, we could legitimately substitute the word *person* or *self*. Christ is asking if being a person is more than just eating. Christ is asking if the body has more importance than just being clothed. Christ obviously expects there to be an innate knowledge within each of God's children that we have a greater destiny and purpose than just to seek fulfillment of needs such as food and clothing.

The Birds of the Air
In this discourse, Christ is trying to lead us out of our narrow vision caused by perceived needs to see material

things in the larger context of how God sees them. In the next verse Christ says:

> *Look at the birds of the air, that they do not sow, neither do they reap, nor gather into barns, and yet your heavenly Father feeds them. Are you not worth much more than they? Matthew 6:26*

Christ observes that Father feeds the birds without them sowing, reaping, and storing their excess food for hard times. Christ argues by a rhetorical question that God's children are of greater value than the birds. Therefore, we should believe that Father has plans for us that do not require sowing, reaping and storage of provisions for the future either. This is important. While sowing and reaping is a principle of financial increase that will be examined in this series of books, Christ tells us here that sowing finances and reaping finances is not a prerequisite to experience Father's care of us in our basic needs of clothing and food. Father cares for us not because we *do something* but because we *are something*. We are His beloved children redeemed by the precious blood of Christ.

Changing Your Height
Anxiety and faith are opposites. Christ is calling us to deal with anxiety in our lives. Obviously, we must have the capacity to successfully deal with anxiety or Christ would not be warning us about it. Christ reminds us that anxiety over needs does not have any power to change our situation by asking another rhetorical question.

And which of you by being anxious can add a single cubit to his life's span? Matthew 6:27

Christ asks if being anxious can add a single cubit to a life's span. The Greek word here for life's span is *helikia*. It primarily is used to describe the age of a person and is related to a person's physical height. A loose translation of this verse would be *being anxious will not make you grow an inch taller*. The point is that God alone can change such things and being anxious about things that you cannot change is a waste of energy.

The Lilies of the Field
Christ then returns to the mundane things that are the basis of our needs in this passage. He says:

And why are you anxious about clothing? Observe how the lilies of the field grow; they do not toil nor do they spin, yet I say to you that even Solomon in all his glory did not clothe himself like one of these.
Matthew 6:28-29

Christ again compares our situation with how Father deals with nature. Father has a plan for the lilies' needs. The lily has all that it needs to grow and become all that it was created to be. All that the plant needs is available when the lily needs it. The lily neither produces nor works for what it needs. Father provides in advance all that the lily needs so that it can become what it was intended in creation. Christ continues His thoughts about plants. He says:

But if God so arrays the grass of the field, which is alive today and tomorrow is thrown into the furnace, will He not much more do so for you, O men of little faith? Matthew 6:30

Christ again argues that God's children are of greater value than plants like the lily that have such a short span of life. If God has a plan for plants to become all that He created them to be, then Father must have a financial plan to meet the needs of His children. If God has already planned and provided in advance for the lily's needs, then much more His care and provision for His own children.

The Basic Needs of Food and Clothing
Christ then summarizes the situation of the basic needs of eating, drinking and clothing. He says:

Do not be anxious then, saying, "What shall we eat?" or "What shall we drink?" or "With what shall we clothe ourselves?" Matthew 6:31

Eating, drinking and clothing are three very basic needs. It is noteworthy that Christ does not mention shelter here. Christ does teach on shelter in other places in the Gospel of Matthew. Christ requires His disciples to be willing to leave their homes for His sake and the sake of the Gospel. He tells them to stay with the first honorable person that offers them lodging as they preach, cast out demons and heal the sick. However, no matter where believers seek shelter, they will still have the need to eat, drink and be clothed as they serve Christ.

76

Father Knows Your Needs

Christ then tells them why they should not be anxious about these things.

> *For all these things the Gentiles eagerly seek; for your heavenly Father knows that you need all these things. Matthew 6:32*

Christ first reminds them that Gentiles eagerly seek these things. This is a way of reminding them that they, His disciples, are different. The Gentiles that Christ is speaking about are without God. The Gospel has not reached them. They know of no gracious God to help them and therefore anxiety for them is reasonable. However, the disciples have received their Messiah. They are now children of God by faith in Jesus Christ. They now have a Father in Heaven that knows exactly what they need and will not fail them. Therefore, anxiety for the sons and daughters of God the Father makes no sense at all.

Conditions for Receiving Needs from Father

Christ then gives the conditions for receiving supply for our needs from Father. He says:

> *But seek first His kingdom and His righteousness; and all these things shall be added to you. Matthew 6:33*

Here is the condition. Either we anxious seek to meet our needs or we seek Christ's kingdom. We cannot do both. We cannot serve God and mammon. We cannot serve two masters. Our spiritual eye cannot focus on two things at the same time. We cannot lay up treasures on earth and in heaven at the same time. Our heart cannot be in two places. The only condition is where our heart is.

The Greek word that is translated *kingdom* in the above verse is *basileia*. It is an abstract noun that denotes sovereignty, royal power and dominion. In this passage it means *the sphere of God's rule*. Christ is encouraging us to seek the rule of God over us first and then God will meet our needs. This is consistent with the Lord's prayer where He teaches us to pray... *thy kingdom come, thy will be done on earth as it is in Heaven.* Christ is encouraging His hearers to seek God's rule over them on earth by seeking the kingdom. Christ is not encouraging us to seek Heaven but His rule over us on earth. If we are ruled by Christ on the earth, then going to Heaven when we die is no longer an issue. *What other eternal destiny could there be for God's children who faithfully serve Christ as their Savior and Lord?*

There is a second thing in this verse that we are encouraged to seek. It is *His righteousness*. The Greek word that is translated righteousness here is *diakaiosene*. This word primarily means *right action*. This word is used to describe God and means essentially His faithfulness and truthfulness in His dealings with humanity. God always has *right actions* towards humanity. Christ also uses this word to describe anything that is good, right or just in itself, and whatever conforms to the revealed will of God. In this sense, it has an opposite meaning to *sinful*. *Sinful* would mean *wrong actions*.

Christ sometimes describes as *righteous* those things that God requires of man, such as giving to the poor, prayer, fasting and the duty of self-control. These are *right actions*. Where the word *righteousness* becomes a little more difficult to understand is how it is used in Paul's writings. Paul tells us that faith in Christ allows God to *reckon or impute righteousness* to a believer. Not only does *righteousness* mean *right actions* but also it means *a state of righteousness*. In other words, God declares us *righteous* on the basis of faith in Christ. God declares that our sins, our wrong actions are forgiven. God declares that we are in a state of righteousness on the basis of faith in Christ. Our faith in Christ through His atoning work at the cross allows God to impute Christ's righteousness to us. This imputed righteousness in Christ then allows us to live out righteousness in right actions, empowered by the Holy Spirit. However, Christ seems to be using this word in the verse above in a more simple sense. Christ is simply saying that we should seek God rule over us and seek to do what God would consider *right actions*. Seeking to do right actions should not be misunderstood as doing right actions. The condition is *seeking* the kingdom and His righteousness. God has made it a matter of the heart and not works. Therefore, anyone can qualify at any moment by simple repentance. They can change their attitude and make the kingdom and His righteousness their priority. At that moment, they qualify to receive from Father without any works. Failure to repent simply means that they have chosen to rely upon themselves and the world's anxious way of dealing with needs.

The Greek word that is translated first in the above verse is *proton*. It is an adverb and is the neuter of the adjective *protos*. It means *the first of time, place or order*. It is the opposite of *the last*. It is sometimes translated *chiefly*. It does not mean to list thing and put God's Kingdom at the top and then to select a second and third priority to seek after seeking God's Kingdom. Rather it means to palce Christ's Kingdom and the central, most important thing in all matters. It means to make the rule of God over us the preeminent thing in all matters. When we do this, then Father will supply our needs. Christ sums up His command in light of Father's care for us. He says:

> *Therefore do not be anxious for tomorrow; for tomorrow will care for itself. Each day has enough trouble of its own. Matthew 6:34*

There is not need to store resources for future needs. Father will take care of us tomorrow. Five times in this passage, Christ has told us not to be anxious about our needs in the future. There is no need to borrow trouble from the future. The future will take care of itself because Father will be there and taking care of us. Father did not intend for us to consider our needs beyond the present. This is radically in conflict with the world's anxious concerns. He says that each day has enough trouble to deal with. The word *trouble* is translated from the Greek word *kakia*. It means *bad* in quality. It is translated with a variety of English words in the New Testament. In this context, it means that each day will have its own challenges to Christ's kingdom over us. Each day we can either choose to be anxious or we can radically trust that Father will supply our needs.

80

There is no need to imagine future challenges that will create anxiety. Father will be just as present to help us in those days also as we seek His Kingdom.

~8~

Beware Every Form of Greed

Jesus warned us about the danger of greed in several places in His teaching. In an exchange with an unidentified person, Christ revealed this about greed:

> *And someone in the crowd said to Him, "Teacher, tell my brother to divide the family inheritance with me." But He said to him, "Man, who appointed Me a judge or arbiter over you?" And He said to them, "Beware, and be on your guard against every form of greed; for not even when one has an abundance does his life consist of his possessions." Luke 8:13-15*

Apparently Christ saw greed in the man's request for Christ to intervene in this financial situation. Christ strongly warns His disciples and us to beware. He warns us that we must be on guard against every form of greed. This, of course, reveals that there is more than one form that greed takes. Some of these forms of greed can be masked and promoted by religious teaching.[1]

---

[1] For an example, see Mark 7:10-13

The Greek word translated *greed* in this passage is *pleonexia*. It is a compound word coming from *pleon* meaning in English *more* and *echo* meaning in English *to have*. It means *a desire to have more*. This word is always used in a negative sense in the New Testament. The opposite of greed, the desire for more, in the New Testament is contentment. Desire for things always grows in proportion with and slightly beyond the ability to obtain them. In other words, I might desire to own a three-bedroom cottage if I am a renter. However, after I own the three-bedroom cottage, my desire grows so that I now desire a larger house in a nicer neighborhood. Greed produces a desire for that thing that is slightly beyond the financial ability at present. This is the reason that many people get into deeper debt as their income grows. They can now afford more and therefore their desire for more grows in proportion with and slightly above their income. They never identify the greed, crucify it, learn to be content with what Father has provided and live within their means.

In many older English versions of the New Testament this Greek word is translated mainly as *covetousness or greediness*. However, in some passages in some older versions, it is translated as *idolatry* or *extortion*.[2] Christ explains why we are to *beware* and be *on guard* about greed. Again Christ says:

> *Beware, and be on your guard against every form of greed; for not even when one has an abundance does his life consist of his possessions.*

---

[2] Vines, pg. 244-245 "Covet, Covetous, Covetousness"

Christ says that our life does not consist of possessions. There is a danger of over-spiritualizing what Christ is saying here. What He is saying is rather simple. The Greek word for *life* here is *zoe*. This word describes the life principle that all animals, men and God all share. Christ is saying that a man's life principle, his existence, his essence, is not changed one iota by an abundance of possessions or money. A billionaire breathes in and out, his heart beats, his thoughts come and go, he sleeps, he eats, he can experience fear, faith, sorrow and joy just like the beggar down the street from him. His life principle is just the same as the beggar. Howard Hughes was one of the wealthiest men who have ever lived. Before his death, he was tormented by many strange phobias. After his death, the executor of his estate was asked how much money that he had left behind. He responded by saying "all of it". We don't get to take it with us and it doesn't have any power to give us life while we are living. Thinking that wealth can produce anything of life or change the inner experience, or create a sense of security, is a deceptive snare that many Christians fall into. Greed, therefore, misdirects a life into pursuits that will disappoint, wound and frustrate. Christ illustrates this by a parable in this discussion of greed. He says in the next verse:

And He told them a parable, saying, "The land of a certain rich man was very productive. And he began reasoning to himself, saying, 'What shall I do, since I have no place to store my crops?' And he said, 'This is what I will do: I will tear down my barns and build larger ones, and there I will store all my grain and my goods." Luke 8:16-18

85

This seems like a reasonable thing for the rich man to do. However, it is not the only thing he could have done. The fact that storing the excess produce appears to be his only thought is revealing. It reveals greed. He could have righteously given the abundance away to the poor. He was _already_ a rich man. He didn't need the excess that could have helped others. A righteous man would have thought of this possibility since the Bible is full of references to the responsibilities of the rich to help the poor. This greedy rich man chose rather to become richer. The next verse reveals his inward motivation and his lack of insight about wealth.

> _And I will say to my soul, "Soul, you have many goods laid up for many years to come; take your ease, eat, drink and be merry."' Luke 8:19_

The rich man thought that having additional wealth would make him more secure. He thought that more would produce a life of ease and happiness. He forgot one important thing; that he, a very bad steward, would have to face God who truly owned all things. He forgot the one thing that is absolutely predictable. That one thing was that he would die and face God in judgment.

> _"But God said to him, 'You fool! This very night your soul is required of you; and now who will own what you have prepared?' Luke 8:20_

This fool had sought to prepare for a life of ease and security but instead he faced God sooner than he had expected and he was completely unprepared spiritually.

Foolishly, he had prepared for the fleeting temporal and ignored the eternal. He had entirely wasted his efforts in obtaining and storing more and more. He was living a misdirected life because of greed. Christ sums up this situation for His disciples by saying:

> *"So is the man who lays up treasure for himself, and is not rich toward God." And He said to His disciples, "For this reason I say to you, do not be anxious for your life, as to what you shall eat; nor for your body, as to what you shall put on. For life is more than food, and the body than clothing." Luke 8:21-23*

Christ succinctly tells us that like the foolish rich man in this parable, we can lay up treasure for ourselves and then not be rich toward God. A key phrase in this is *for himself.* It is possible to have wealth without selfish intent, without greediness, without seeking a life of ease. It is possible for God's wealth to be in the hands of His true stewards who lavishly give and support Christ's causes. However, to have wealth and not be rich toward God is extremely foolish.

The Relationship Between Greed and Anxiety

Christ reveals in these verses the clear relationship between greed and anxiety. Anxiety is a subtle form of fear. Anxiety manifests itself with feelings and thoughts that if we do not take care of ourselves then we will not be taken care of. If this fear is left to grow unchecked, then greed will be one of its fruits. We will try unsuccessfully to resolve anxious feelings of insecurity by acquiring more and more property and wealth. Christ reminds us in the next verses that our Father has a much better financial plan for us.

At this point in this passage, there is some repetition of ideas that are found elsewhere in Christ's teaching. This is not unexpected. After all, Christ preached on finances many times in His ministry. The ongoing use of particular truths and particular illustrations in several different contexts and situations is only logical. In the next verses, Christ will repeat some of these important truths. Since the Holy Spirit has seen fit to emphasize these truths by having them recorded more than once in a very different teaching, this book will also discuss them again.

Consider the Ravens

The next verse has some of the same truths concerning God's care of birds that were found in Matthew's Gospel although the context was different. That context was the Sermon on the Mount. This context is Christ's discussion about greed. Christ says:

> *Consider the ravens, for they neither sow nor reap; and they have no storeroom nor barn; and yet God feeds them; how much more valuable you are than the birds! Luke 8:24*

Christ reminds us that God has revealed His financial plan for us in the lives of birds. First of all, birds do not sow and reap and yet God cares for them. God's care for our needs is not based on our sowing and reaping but rather our great value as sons and daughters of God. In other words, God does not care for us because we give to Christian ministries or to the poor even though these are important things to do for Christ. He provides for us because we are His children. Christ reminds us that the birds, unlike the foolish rich man, do not store up valuables for the future and yet God feeds them. We need not store valuables either. Christ is obviously encouraging us to live without anxiety over our financial futures. He reminds us that we are _much more_ valuable than the birds and if God takes care of them how _much more_ will He care for us, His children. The spirits of anxiety and fear lie to us that this is not so. Christ continues to remind His disciples and us of important facts about life and its relationship to finances. He says:

> _And which of you by being anxious can add a single cubit to his life's span? If then you cannot do even a very little thing, why are you anxious about other matters? Luke 8:25-26_

Christ teaches that many important things are _not_ within our power to control. For instance, we cannot add a single day to our life span. We cannot add an inch to our height. We, therefore, cannot predict what our future needs may or may not be. We may need nothing tomorrow because we are in Heaven awaiting the final resurrection of the dead. Therefore, to be anxious about our financial futures is misguided at best. We may not need anything in the future and if we do our Father will provide it. To waste our lives with no higher intent than producing and storing wealth for some future need that may never appear is foolish. It reveals a lack of faith in the Father's ability to take care of us all through our lives as easily as He takes care of the birds.

Consider the Lilies
Christ reminds the disciples and us of another example of God's care. Christ says:

> *Consider the lilies, how they grow; they neither toil nor spin; but I tell you, even Solomon in all his glory did not clothe himself like one of these. But if God so arrays the grass in the field, which is alive today and tomorrow is thrown into the furnace, how much more will He clothe you, O men of little faith! Luke 8:27-28*

Here Christ reminds us again as He did in Matthew's Gospel that the Father has revealed His financial plan for us in plant life. Consider that plants grow and are provided water, sunlight, and nutrition from the soil without laboring for these things. All that the plant needs is already in place before the plant spouts. If God feeds and provides beautiful clothing for plants like the lily that have no lasting value, then logically He will provide clothing and other needs for His children who are eternally His. We must trust in Father.

Seeking the Kingdom
Christ again sums up what this means for us who are following Him.

> *And do not seek what you shall eat, and what you shall drink, and do not keep worrying. For all these things the nations of the world eagerly seek; but your Father knows that you need these things. But seek for His kingdom, and these things shall be added to you. Luke 8:29-31*

The nations without Christ seek these things and they must in order to survive. However, Father has a tried and true financial system already in place for His child that is based on the hidden abundance in Christ's Kingdom. As we place Christ's interests first, seeking His Kingdom first, then we will experience Father's care in the same way that the plants and the birds do. Father will add all things that we need to survive and prosper in His will. For those who think that receiving supply from Father is difficult. Christ reassures that it is not in the next verse.

Father Gives Us the Kingdom Gladly
The next verse in this passage in Luke's Gospel is not found in Matthew's Gospel. Christ says encouragingly:

Do not be afraid, little flock, for your Father has chosen gladly to give you the kingdom. Luke 8:32

Fear, often in the form of anxiety, is the ongoing issue that faces anyone wishing to walk in the supernatural in finances. Kingdom rule over our finances means that we no longer own anything. It means that we must fully obey the real Owner as stewards. *Do we really believe that Father will take care of us like He does the birds? Do we really believe that Christ is perfectly revealing Father's will? Can it really be this simple?* Christ is commanding radical trust in Father's provision. We must believe what Christ is saying is true and live securely in Christ's promise of Father's care... or we will submit to earthly fears and try to create our own security.

Eternal Purses, Unfailing Treasures
Considering what He has already told us, Christ adds a logical command to the end of this discourse. He says:

> *Sell your possessions and give to charity; make yourselves purses which do not wear out, an unfailing treasure in heaven, where no thief comes near, nor moth destroys. For where your treasure is, there will your heart be also. Luke 8:33-34*

For those who are putting their trust in riches, these must be difficult verses. However for those who are true stewards, this is not difficult at all. A steward knows that he or she is operating from a divine and unlimited financial supply, i.e. *a purse that will not wear out, an unfailing treasure in heaven.* This is truly a place of security since a thief or any earthly circumstance cannot affect this supply negatively. If a command comes to give all, then more supply will come by God's great grace. If our treasure is truly in heaven, then our supply from Father will be unending and reliable.

Our heart's focus will determine our experience. Anxiety, fear and greed are a result of earthly focus. They, in turn, will restrict God's grace in supply and cause us to fail as stewards. Faith, trust and commitment are the result of a heavenly focus. They will cause us to embrace true stewardship. In turn, Father's grace will abound, testimonies of His supply and abundant financing of His kingdom projects and people will be evident. If we *make for ourselves* these kinds of purses by radical trust in Father, we will be blessed.

~9~

Lending to Your Enemies

The distinctive nature of stewardship shows up throughout the teachings of Christ. In a fairly long passage in Luke Chapter 6, Christ encourages His disciples to be completely different from the world in dealing with enemies. He says:

Whoever hits you on the cheek, offer him the other also; and whoever takes away your coat, do not withhold your shirt from him either. Give to everyone who asks of you, and whoever takes away what is yours, do not demand it back. Luke 6:29-30

It is clear that God's view of stewardship is consistently different than what the world would consider to be logical. Here material possessions are forcibly taken and believers are supposed to give voluntarily additional possessions to the one forcibly taking them. Additionally, we are not to demand the possessions back. This transforms the situation from one of abuse to a situation of showing mercy and grace. This requires a clear emotional separation of the believer's heart from the love of money and possessions.

Christ's instruction here is if possessions are taken involuntarily, then we are to let them go with such freedom that we can give other possessions to the one taking them. This has to have a profound effect on the one who was taking the possessions. To this, Christ adds:

> *And just as you want people to treat you, treat them in the same way. Luke 6:31*

This is another expression of that which has been called *the Golden Rule*. An application here would be... *if you want people to freely give to you under bad circumstances, freely give to them under bad circumstances.* This sounds much like *making friends by means of unrighteous mammon*. The relational purpose of money is seen again here. Money and possessions are not given by God to create security in this world. They are given by God to create and strengthen relationships.

Lending to Those Who Love You
Christ continues to speak about the idea of giving voluntarily to the enemy who tries to coerce you. He says:

> *And if you love those who love you, what credit is that to you? For even sinners love those who love them. And if you do good to those who do good to you, what credit is that to you? For even sinners do the same.*
> *Luke 6:32-33*

In this, Christ again tells His disciples in general terms that they are to be very different than a sinner. The sinner loves those who love him. The sinner does good for those who do good for him. Christ's disciples are to love their enemies and do good to those who abuse them. Now in a specific way, Christ tells His disciples how this pertains to loaning money. He says in the next verse:

> *And if you lend to those from whom you expect to receive, what credit is that to you? Even sinners lend to sinners, in order to receive back the same amount.*
> *Luke 6:34*

This is, of course, very radical to most Christians today. The Church has not been taught this. *Why?* Most probably, the primary reasons are ignorance, unbelief and fear. Many are simply ignorant of what stewardship really means. Conversely, those who know that Christ teaches this and do not teach it, fear of man and unbelief is the probable reason. The idea of lending money without expecting to receive anything back is very challenging. However, it is whom we are to lend to that makes this even more wonderfully radical. We are to lend to our enemies.

Being Sons and Daughters of the Most High

Loving our enemies becomes intensely practical as we lend to our enemies expecting nothing in return. Christ says in the next verse.

> *But love your enemies, and do good, and lend, expecting nothing in return; and your reward will be great, and you will be sons of the Most High; for He Himself is kind to ungrateful and evil men. Luke 6:35*

We are to love our enemies in a financial way. Since we are not to expect anything in return, the *lending* here is really free-will *giving*. This is a distinct way to lay up treasures in heaven. Our reward according to Christ will be great. We will be sons and daughters of the Most High God for we will be demonstrating His kindness by acting as He does. This requires a radical trust in Father's provision to live in this way. Christ continues this discourse with some clear reasons that we don't loan to our enemies. He says:

> *Be merciful, just as your Father is merciful. And do not judge and you will not be judged; and do not condemn, and you will not be condemned; pardon, and you will be pardoned. Luke 6:36-37*

We don't lend or give because we are not merciful like our Father is. We don't lend because we have judged and have condemned our enemies. When we do lend, we are showing mercy. We are pardoning those enemies who perhaps deserve condemnation. In doing this, we receive from God pardon as well.

Give and it will Be Given to You
Into this context of lending to enemies, comes an often-misused verse on giving. Christ says:

> *Give, and it will be given to you; good measure, pressed down, shaken together, running over, they will pour into your lap. For by your standard of measure it will be measured to you in return. Luke 6:38*

First of all, we need to notice that this verse is not in a context of giving to the Church, its ministries, or even to the poor. This verse is in a context of *lending to our enemies*. In fact, the context a few verses earlier says that if we give to those that we love and love us, that even sinners do the same. Christ assumes generosity with family members and friends. He is calling us to generosity in situations where we have bad relationships.

Secondly, the verse says that *they will pour into your lap*. The verse doesn't specifically say who the *they* is in this verse that will be giving to those who give to their enemies. However, the context has been about our *enemies* throughout. *Who else could it be?* It would seem that Christ is saying that our *enemies* will be the ones *who pour into our laps*. What Christ seems to be saying here is that we will make friends by freely lending to our enemies. These former enemies, some as friends now, will pour resources into our laps. Again, Christ seems to teach a relational use of money. Certainly, His teaching cuts across anyone's unhealthy desire to create security in this world by means of finances.

Thirdly, the return of resources in this verse is directly related to the *standard of measure* of the believer who was lending originally. The question of how much mercy, how much pardon shown was answered by how much was lent without expecting a return. The amount of mercy revealed by lending an amount of material substance is the measure. In other words, if a small amount was lent or given without expecting return, then a small amount was returned to the believer. If a large amount of mercy was shown financially to the enemy, then a large amount could be expected back. Christ uses four modifiers to relate just how much that the believer who gives to enemies is to receive. Christ says... *good measure, pressed down, shaken together, running over.* All these phrases together reveal a container packed full of abundant provision to the place of overflowing.

Finally, Christ's encouragement here that we will receive an overflowing abundance if we give must be taken in light of what He says about the nature of that giving. Christ tells us to lend to enemies *without expecting anything back* from them. Then later, He tells us to expect that when we give in this way, that we will be given much more resources. Therefore, our motives must remain pure. We give or lend without expecting a return from those that we give to. We are simply obeying Christ as His stewards and seeking to make friends using unrighteous mammon. However, we need to understand that God will cause some of the friends that we make in this way to give back in abundance. However, the timing of our needs and their supply, the particular amounts, and the particular persons involved in God's provision are all thankfully outside of our control. This requires a radical trust of Father's provision and exceedingly pure motives for giving.

Christ has not revealed truth to encourage us to work this process to obtain money. Christ has revealed the process to calm our fears. Christ's teaching encourages us to radical trust of our Father and freedom to use money to make friends.

~10~

Forgive Us
Our Debts

This first book has sought to cover most of what the Lord Jesus Christ has to say about money. In the next three volumes of this series, we will examine what the rest of the New Testament says about money. However, this volume would not be complete without adding one more related subject. Christ often used financial debt to symbolically represent sin. The Lord Jesus Christ often spoke of the forgiveness of sin as the *forgiveness of debt.* For example, Christ spoke of debt in a familiar portion of the two passages known as the Lord's Prayer. He said:

And forgive us our debts, as we also have forgiven our debtors. Matthew 6:2

And in Luke's Gospel:

And forgive us our sins, for we ourselves also forgive everyone who is indebted to us. Luke 4:4a

In both of these statements, Christ used the word *debt* to describe what we *owe* God because of sin. It is interesting that Christ does not say that we owe God a debt for our creation, our lives, or anything else except sin. He also uses *indebted* to describe what people *owe* us on the basis of their sins against us personally. In either case, forgiveness releases the *indebted* person from their *debt* either to God or to another person. Forgiveness of sins means that we no longer owe God a debt. Luke records a short parable where Christ says:

> *"A certain moneylender had two debtors: one owed five hundred denarii, and the other fifty. When they were unable to repay, he graciously forgave them both. Which of them therefore will love him more?" Simon answered and said, "I suppose the one whom he forgave more." And He said to him," You have judged correctly. " Luke 7:41-43*

In this parable, Christ symbolized the Father by the moneylender. Those who owe amounts of money to the moneylender symbolize sinners. The sinner with the greater sins is the greater debtor. In other words, forgiving a debt of money is being compared to the forgiveness of sin. Additionally, Christ a point of the parable is love. The purpose of forgiveness of debt, sin or money, is relational. It causes the one who is forgiven debt to love the one who forgives. This is consistent with Christ's teaching in other places where the relational element of finances is exalted.

Parable of the Unmerciful Servant
Peter asked Christ an important question that reveals more about sin, debt, and forgiveness. In Christ's answer to Peter's question, He put sin into the context of debt once again. Another relational truth is discovered here.

Then Peter came and said to Him, "Lord, how often shall my brother sin against me and I forgive him? Up to seven times?" Jesus said to him, "I do not say to you, up to seven times, but up to seventy times seven."
Matthew 18:21-22

Peter wanted to know what the limits are on forgiving others. Christ's answer revealed that there are no limits. We are to keep forgiving regardless of the behavior of the offending person. Christ illustrated this by comparing the forgiveness of debt to forgiveness of sin. He says in the next verses:

"For this reason the kingdom of heaven may be compared to a certain king who wished to settle accounts with his slaves." And when he had begun to settle them, there was brought to him one who owed him ten thousand talents." Matthew 18: 23-24

The king symbolizes God in this parable. This king has servants who owe him a financial debt. Christ will again relate financial debt to sin in the parable. The king wishes to settle accounts with these servants. Of course, we will all eventually have a final accounting with God. One of two things will happen. We will either unhappily account for our existing debt of sin or Christ will have already paid in full our debt of sin. In this parable, the servant cannot possibly pay the large debt that he owed. Christ said:

"But since he did not have the means to repay, his lord commanded him to be sold, along with his wife and

children and all that he had, and repayment to be made." Matthew 18:25

Because the servant cannot pay his large debt, the king commands dire consequences. The servant and his family will be sold into slavery. All their belongings will be taken from them and sold as well. The servant reacts to these consequences and humbles himself before the king. Christ said:

> *"The slave therefore falling down, prostrated himself before him, saying, 'Have patience with me, and I will repay you everything.'" Matthew 18:26*

The servant asks the king for more time to repay this large debt. However, because the king feels compassion for him, he gives him much more than just time to repay the debt. Christ said:

> *"And the lord of that slave felt compassion and released him and forgave him the debt."Matthew 18:27*

Instead of more time to repay the debt, the king releases him and forgives him the debt. However, the now forgiven servant does not reveal the same sort of compassion to a fellow servant. Christ said:

> *"But that slave went out and found one of his fellow slaves who owed him a hundred denarii; and he seized him and began to choke him, saying, 'Pay back what you owe.' Matthew 18:28*

The now forgiven servant finds someone who owes him a very small amount of money and forcefully demands payment. Christ said:

>*"So his fellow slave fell down and began to entreat him, saying, ' Have patience with me and I will repay you. '"Matthew 18:29*

The fellow slave reacts in a similar manner to the demand for payment. In this case, since the amount is much smaller, there is real hope for repayment. However, the forgiven slave is unwilling to wait for repayment. Christ said:

>*"He was unwilling however, but went and threw him in prison until he should pay back what was owed."*
>*Matthew 18:30*

The forgiven servant has the slave incarcerated until repayment is made of the small debt. When the forgiven servant's behavior toward his fellow slave is known, there is a reaction. Christ said:

>*"So when his fellow slaves saw what had happened, they were deeply grieved and came and reported to their lord all that had happened." Matthew 18:31*

The king hears about the forgiven servant's behavior, summons him and reacts strongly to the news. Christ said:

>*"Then summoning him, his lord said to him, 'You wicked slave, I forgave you all that debt because you*

entreated me. Should you not also have had mercy on your fellow slave, even as I had mercy on you?'" Matthew 18:32-33

The king called the forgiven servant a *wicked* slave because of his failure to show mercy to the other slave. The king's logic was clear. Someone who has been shown great mercy by forgiveness of a large debt should forgive everyone who owes him a smaller debt. The king then commanded another dire consequence. Christ said:

"And his lord, moved with anger, handed him over to the torturers until he should repay all that was owed him." Matthew 18:34

First of all, the forgiveness of the large debt is revoked. The servant again owes the debt. Secondly, the servant is turned over to *the torturers* until repayment is made. The Greek word translated *torturers* here is *basanistes.* This Greek word describes a jailor that uses torture to elicit responses. In this case, the servant will be tortured until the debt is paid. Since the debt is so large and therefore impossible to pay back, the torture will go on indefinitely. Christ then makes the primary point of the entire parable. He says:

"So shall My heavenly Father also do to you, if each of you does not forgive his brother from your heart." Matthew 18:35

God the Father will do what the king did in this parable if we fail to forgive others. It is important to notice that the forgiveness of others is not the issue at first. The king *first* forgives the servant's debt and then the forgiven servant is expected to forgive others. Forgiveness is freely given and there is *no* qualifying condition of forgiving others. We are not forgiven *because* we forgive others. We are shown mercy by God because of faith in Christ's sacrifice and *then* we forgive others. However, the forgiveness of our debt of sin will be revoked if we fail to forgive others. This makes forgiveness of others an issue of discipleship and not an issue of evangelism. Christ will save, heal and deliver people *before* they forgive others. They simply will not be able to maintain what they receive from Christ if they fail to forgive others in the days, weeks and months that follow. This means that a responsibility of being forgiven is forgiving others.

The Certificate of Debt Canceled
Not only does Christ reveal the power and responsibility of forgiveness but the apostle Paul also addresses this issue. He reveals that Father has dealt finally and completely with the debt of sin that we owed Him. Paul writes:

> *He (Father) made you alive together with Him (Christ), having forgiven us all our transgressions, having canceled out the certificate of debt consisting of decrees against us and which was hostile to us; and He (Father) has taken it out of the way, having nailed it to the cross. Colossians 2:13b-14 (words in parenthesis added by author for clarity)*

What Paul is telling us here is the Law of Moses had *decrees against us*. Violations of the Law of Moses caused us to be indebted to God and a written certificate expresses this debt. The Greek word here that is translated *certificate of debt* is *cheirographa*. It is a common word in ancient Greek writings and describes a financial document. This would be identical in purpose to a promissory note today. Paul also reveals what was written on this certificate. It had the decrees in the Law of Moses written on it.

Paul tells us that this certificate of debt to God has been *cancelled*. The Greek word here is *exaleipho*. It means *blotted out, erased,* or *wiped off.* In other words, there is no longer a record of what we owe to God. The certificate has been *forgiven, cancelled, blotted out, erased,* and *wiped off.* Additionally, Paul tells us that Father has taken it (the certificate) out of the way. This phrase comes from the Greek word *airo* that means to *lift up, to bear,* or *to take away.* This word is in the perfect tense, which means that it emphasizes the permanence of the removal of the debt. It emphasizes that the debt cannot be presented again.

Finally, Paul tells us exactly *where* the *blotted out* and *erased* certificate of debt has been *taken out of the way.* It has been nailed to the cross of Christ. When Christ died on the cross, the Law of Moses was fulfilled and no longer has any power over us. Christ has paid in full our debt to God. The debt has been completely erased and taken out of the way. We have no debt to God to repay even if it were possible. We love Him, not out of obligation, but out of gratitude. This is an important point and will be revisited when we consider giving and receiving financial blessings from God in future volumes of this series of books.

What are the implications of Christ, Paul and others using the idea of financial debt to describe sin? First of all, since financial debt is a biblical picture of sin, it is obvious that Christians should seek to be free from all financial debt. God will surely help them obtain freedom from financial debt. Both Old and New Testaments agree with the wisdom of being debt free. In a context about paying taxes, the apostle Paul wrote in Romans:

> _Owe nothing to anyone except to love one another; for he who loves his neighbor has fulfilled the law. Romans 13:8_

We don't serve God or others out of obligation but out of love. Debt makes us serve Christ out of obligation. Debt produces shame and guilt within us. Debt makes us think and behave like unwilling slaves rather than sons and daughters of God who freely serve Christ out of love.

Secondly, it is clear that there is _not_ a direct relationship between forgiveness and being financially debt free. Notice what the risen Christ says to the Church at Smyrna:

> _"I know your tribulation and your poverty (but you are rich)..." Revelation 2:9a_

There are many who are experiencing Father's forgiveness and yet are in serious financial debt. There are also others who are extremely wealthy in terms of possessions and financial resources and yet are still in spiritual debt to God because of sin. They are spiritually poor. Hear what Christ says to the Church at Laodicea:

Because you say, "I am rich, and have become wealthy, and have need of nothing," and you do not know that you are wretched and miserable and poor and blind and naked. I advise you to buy from Me gold refined by fire, that you may become rich, and white garments, that you may clothe yourself, and that the shame of your nakedness may not be revealed; and eye salve to anoint your eyes, that you may see. Revelation 3:17-18

In light of this, no one should ever condemn those who are struggling financially as if they were failing God. Believers get in financial debt for good reasons as well as bad ones. Some are seriously in debt because of lengthy medical care of a loved one. Some of these reasons for debt are not in their control. God does not condemn them and neither should we. However, since Christ has paid in full our debt to God, it seems reasonable to expect that Christ will help us deal with financial debt. After all, when a man or woman becomes Christ's steward, not only do they acknowledge that all their wealth and possessions belong to God but they also must acknowledge that their debt belongs to God as well. Father has abundant resources to deal with debt in the lives of His true stewards.

Thirdly, the foundation of all that God does in a believer's life is forgiveness. Everyone needs to know that Father forgives freely because of what Christ has done at the cross. Experiencing forgiveness is the beginning of stewardship. We give our lives, past, present and future into the care of Father. Our past is cleansed. Our present is made new in Christ. Our future is secured in hope of the resurrection of the dead. There can be no true stewardship without the transformation that forgiveness works in us. We are led by the Spirit of Christ from obligation to love, from legalism to grace, from bondage to freedom, and from slavery to sonship.

Did you find this book interesting,
informative and challenging?

You will find the other books in the
Paid in Full
financial series much the same.

You may order them securely online at

www.allnationsmin.org

or by calling
All Nations Publications at

1-817-514-0653